Mental Maths Practice 6

Teacher's Book

Peter Clarke

Christina Rossiter

Heinemann

Introduction

Children need to develop mental strategies as all mathematical problems involve some form of mental activity. Pupils will be unable to complete practical investigations successfully unless they can hold mental images in their heads. To build these up and learn to manipulate them flexibly takes practice.

Pupils at all ages and abilities have their own mental images. It is the responsibility of the teacher to provide opportunities for pupils to discuss these images. Only through discussion does the teacher develop an insight into pupils' mental computational strategies and do the pupils themselves need this opportunity to articulate their abstract mental processes.

Using this book

This book is a resource for practice and consolidation, from which pupils are able to enhance their understanding of strategies for mental calculations. It is assumed that teachers will have taught the basis strategies and concepts covered. The range of mental maths activities included here is appropriate for 10–11 year olds, though individual teachers or schools may decide to use it for other year groups (e.g. the more able 9–10 year olds.

There are 30 exercises, to be used across the school year providing ten per term, with each set of ten focusing on a similar range of concepts. This allows for consolidation before moving on.

Each exercise is further divided into four sections, A-D, so each section can be treated as approximately ten minutes's daily practice. Sets A and C provide fifteen calculations covering place value and whole number, and the four operations, with particular reference to the signs and symbols associated with these calculations. At the end of each section is an extension activity for those pupils who finish quickly, often in the form of an investigation. Pencil and paper may be used to support the mental process within these investigations. Sets B and D include a range of word-associated problems, many in the context of shape, space and measures.

Mental calculation strategies

Pupils' mental strategies are based on an awareness of the number system, and number operations, their recall of number facts, and the ability to make sense of number problems. A range of strategies which pupils need to be taught in order to refine their methods of calculating are provided below:

Addition and subtraction

- When adding two sets and the size of each set is known, don't count the quantities.
- Start with the largest number first
- Count on or back in repeated steps
- Know that 7 + 2 is the same as 2 + 7
- Know that the difference between two numbers can be approached by looking at what needs to be added to the smaller number to make the larger one.
- Use two stages to add 9 (i.e. + 10 – 1) and subtract 9 (i.e.+ 10 + 1)
- Use two stages to add 11 (i.e. + 10 + 1) and subtract 11 (i.e. –10 – 1)
- Know that pairs of digits can be manipulated without affecting the total, e.g. 69 + 21 is the same as 70 + 20, thus helping to create more 'friendly' pairs
- Know doubles, e.g. 3 + 3
- Know near doubles, based on doubles already known, e.g. 3 + 4 is one more than 3 + 3
- Know facts that are two apart and can be transformed into doubles, e.g. 9 + 11 = 10 + 10

Patterns

e.g.	8 + 0 = 8	5 + 2 = 7
	7 + 1 = 8	2 + 5 = 7
	6 + 2 = 8	7 – 5 = 2
	5 + 3 = 8	7 – 2 = 5

Multiples of 10

- Adding any multiple of 10 to a single digit number does not change the unit number, e.g. 6 + 2 = 8
  6 + 12 = 18
- Adding any multiple of 10 to a number does not change the unit number, e.g. 16 + 20 = 36
  16 + 30 = 46

Partitioning into 5 and 10 when adding

- Partition 6, 7, 8 or 9 into '5 and something', e.g.

$$\begin{array}{ccc} 8 & + & 6 \\ (5+3) & + & (5+1) \\ (5+5) & + & (3+1) \\ 10 & + & 4 \\ & 14 & \end{array}$$

- Partition into '10 and something', e.g.

$$\begin{array}{ccc} 16 & + & 13 \\ (10+10) & + & (6+3) \\ 20 & + & 9 \\ & 29 & \end{array}$$

Multiplication and division

- Know that 3 + 3 + 3 + 3 is the same as 4 × 3 (or 3 × 4)
- Know that every division fact has a corresponding multiplication fact, involving the same three numbers
- Use two stages to multiply by 5, i.e. ×10, ÷2; and two stages to divide by 5, i.e. ÷10, × 2.

Progression and continuity

This book and the others in this series, contain mental maths exercises that have been carefully planned and graded. There are opportunities to revisit aspects of mental recall as well as cover new concepts. This spiral approach reinforces and develops mental strategies, both between exercises, and from one book to the next, placing an emphasis on continued accuracy, and progression. By this stage, although mental fluency is clearly the focus, you may decide to allow pupils to use pencil and paper or a calculator, alongside the mental calculation.

Language of mathematics

Mental Maths Practice provides an opportunity for teachers to develop mental maths, presenting pupils with aural exercises, or by marking an exercise with the class and asking individual pupils to articulate their mental methods of computation. It is important for pupils to become good communicators of mathematics, able to clarify observations and discoveries, and communicate their findings to others. Teachers must use a range of appropriate vocabulary: whilst accepting pupils' early mathematical vocabulary, they should also assist them in developing more formal mathematical language as it is required.

Exercise 1

A

1 $9 \times 8 =$ 72

2 4569, [4570], 4571, 4572

3 $23 + 23 + 12 =$ 58

4 $265 + 423 =$ 688

5 $12 \times 6 =$ 72

6 $48 -$ [23] $= 25$

7 $16 \div 4 =$ 4

8 $\frac{1}{2} + \frac{1}{4} = \frac{3}{4}$

9 $3^2 =$ 9

10 3285, 3295, [3305], 3315

11 $-5 + 7 =$ 2

12 $\frac{1}{4} = 0{\cdot}$[25] $=$ [25]%

13 $(5 \times 4) - 6 =$ 14

14 $85 \div 5 =$ 17

15 25% of 120 = 30

Copy and complete.

+	32	29	16	54
17	49	46	33	71
23	55	52	39	77
45	77	74	61	99
28	60	57	44	82

B

1 Write 10 201 in words.
ten thousand two hundred and one

2 Round 1785 to the nearest 1000. 1800

3 What value has the 5 in 15 217?
5000 or 5 thousands

4 Is the answer to 767 + 426 nearer 1100 or 1200? 1200

5 Give 2 factors of 24.
any two from 1, 2, 3, 4, 6, 8, 12, or 24

6 Simon builds a house using 36 cubes. 25% are red. How many is this? 9

7 Name a prime number between 1 and 5.
2 or 3

8 $4^2 + 3 =$ 19

9 Sandra read 216 pages of her book last week and 385 pages this week. How many pages has she read altogether? 601

10 Chocolate biscuits come in packets of 6. Gita buys 8 packets. How many biscuits does she get? 48

11 I spend £8·78, and pay with a £10 note. How much change do I get? £1·22

12 Put these decimals in order, smallest first: 1·3, 1·5, 1·25 1·25, 1·3, 1·5

13 Is an angle of 108° acute or obtuse? obtuse

14 Joanne has 35 sweets. If she shared them between 8 children, how many would they have each? 4 r 3

15 A fairground ride costs 75p. How many rides can Jude have for £3? 4

C

1 $3 \times 0 =$ 0

2 5272, 5271, 5270, 5269

3 $58 - 12 - 24 =$ 22

4 $237 - 116 =$ 121

5 8 $\times 12 = 96$

6 $32 \div$ 4 $= 8$

7 $46 + 23 =$ 69

8 $\frac{1}{2} - \frac{1}{4} = \frac{1}{4}$

9 $6^2 + 8 =$ 44

10 4537, 4532, 4527, 4522

11 $-8 + 3 + 2 =$ −3

12 $\frac{9}{3} =$ 3

13 $(3 \times 9) + 8 =$ 35

14 $90 \div 5 =$ 18

15 $\frac{3}{4}$ of $16 =$ 12

Draw 3 different shapes with an area of 9 cm^2

D

1 Write fifty-six thousand seven hundred and fifty-one in numerals. 56 751

2 15 thousand + 6 units + 4 tens + 2 hundreds = 15 246

3 Put these numbers in order, smallest first: 12 605, 2915, 12 506. 2915, 12 506, 12 605

4 Estimate the answer to 19×6. 114

5 The temperature is 2°C, overnight it drops 2 degrees.
What is the new temperature? 0°C

6 What are the next two multiples of 9?
36, 45, 54, 63

7 What is the volume of a cube with sides measuring 2 cm? 8 cm^3

8 What number multiplied by itself gives 81? 9

9 250 people are in a queue to see a film. The cinema holds 520 people. How many more people will be let in? 270

10 A cardigan has 9 buttons. If 72 buttons are used, how many cardigans is this? 8

11 Complete the ratio, 1:7, 12:84

12 I buy two bunches of flowers at £1·50, how much change do I get from £10? £7·00

13 What is this shape?

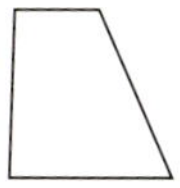

trapezium

14 Is a metre longer or shorter than a yard?
longer

15 There are four cubes in a bag, three are red, one is blue. What chance have I got of pulling out a red one? 3 in 4 or $\frac{3}{4}$

Exercise 2

A

1 $7 \times 6 =$ 42

2 3754, 3755, [3756], 3757

3 $65 + 23 + 11 =$ 99

4 $436 + 423 =$ 859

5 $12 \times 9 =$ 108

6 $69 -$ [37] $= 32$

7 $30 \div 6 =$ 5

8 $\frac{1}{6} + \frac{2}{3} = \frac{5}{6}$

9 $4^2 =$ 16

10 4629, 4637, 4645, [4653]

11 $-6 + 9 =$ 3

12 $\frac{1}{2} = 0\cdot$[5] = [50]%

13 $(3 \times 9) - 7 =$ 20

14 $144 \div 9 =$ 16

15 50% of 180 = 90

What are the co-ordinates for this shape?

(2,0) (3,1) (1,3) (3,5) (2,6) (5,6) (4,5) (6,3) (4,1) (5,0)

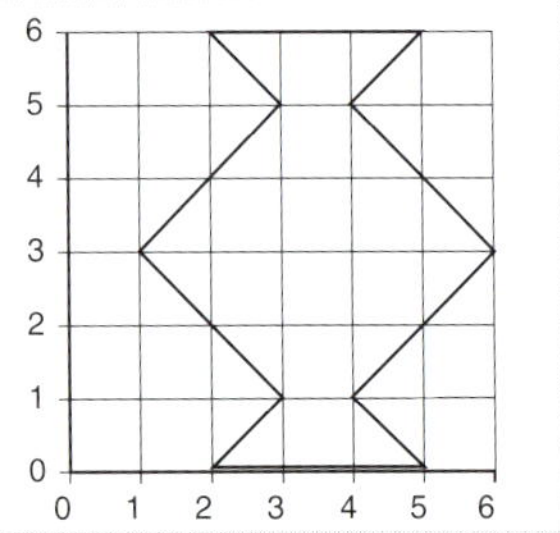

B

1 Write 18 007 in words.
eighteen thousand and seven

2 Round 18 709 to the nearest 1000. 19 000

3 What value has the 3 in 20 309?
300 or 3 hundreds

4 Is the answer to 526 + 787 nearer 1200 or 1300? 1300

5 Give two factors of 20.
any 2 from 1, 2, 4, 5, 10 and 20

6 Jenny is making a model with 20 cubes. 20% of the cubes are green. How many is this? 4

7 Name a prime number between 4 and 10.
5 or 7

8 $6^2 + 8 =$ 44

9 Paula buys a birthday card which costs £1·25 and a present which costs £5·99. How much does she spend in total? £7·24

10 If there are six eggs in each box, how many eggs in 9 boxes? 54

11 I spend £7·62, and pay with a £10 note. How much is my change? £2·38

12 Put these decimals in order, smallest first: 2·7, 2·69, 2·79 2·69, 2·7, 2·79

13 Is an angle of 32° acute or obtuse? acute

14 Stevie has 43 apples. If she shared them between 9 children, how many would they have each? 4 r 7

15 Ice-creams cost 65p. How many could Tony get for £1·95? 3

C

1 $3 \times 4 =$ 12

2 4631, 4630, [4629], 4628

3 $64 - 12 - 21 =$ 31

4 $468 - 234 =$ 234

5 [7] $\times 13 = 91$

6 $42 \div$ [7] $= 6$

7 $52 + 37 =$ 89

8 $\frac{3}{4} - \frac{1}{2} = \frac{1}{4}$

9 $3^2 + 6 =$ 15

10 2341, 2335, [2329], 2323

11 $-9 + 6 + 2 =$ −1

12 $\frac{12}{4} =$ 3

13 $(4 \times 6) + 7 =$ 31

14 $112 \div 7 =$ 16

15 $\frac{2}{3}$ of $15 =$ 10

Can you make 51 using + and × and all five numbers only once?

3	6
4	15
	14

$(3 \times 6) + 4 + 15 + 14 = 51$

D

1 Write forty thousand one hundred and eight in numerals. 40 108

2 21 thousand + 2 units + 6 hundreds + 1 ten = 21 612

3 Put these numbers in order, largest first: 23 004, 2304, 24 003 24 003, 23 004, 2304

4 Estimate the answer to 19×8. 152

5 The temperature is 3°C. Overnight it drops 4 degrees. What is the new temperature −1°C

6 What are the next two multiples of 7? 70, 77, [84], [91]

7 What is the volume of a cube with sides measuring 3 cm? 27 cm^3

8 What number multiplied by itself gives 64? 8

9 There are 642 people staying at a holiday centre. At the weekend 387 people leave. How many people are left at the centre? 255

10 A bookshelf is filled with books whose spines are 4 cm wide. The bookshelf is 52 cm long. How many books will it hold? 13

11 Complete the ratio, 1:5 6:[30]

12 I buy three magazines at £1·45 each. How much change do I get from £10? £5·65

13 What is this shape?

a parallelogram

14 Is a litre more or less than a pint? more

15 There are six cubes in a bag. There are 2 blue cubes, 2 green cubes and 2 red cubes. What chance do I have of pulling out a green cube? 2 in 6 or 1 in 3

Exercise 3

A

1 $4 \times 9 =$ 36

2 6997, 6998, 6999, [7000]

3 $53 + 21 + 33 =$ 107

4 $375 + 423 =$ 798

5 $12 \times 7 =$ 84

6 $57 -$ [45] $= 12$

7 $45 \div 5 =$ 9

8 $\frac{1}{5} + \frac{2}{10} = \frac{[4]}{[10]}$ or $\frac{[2]}{[5]}$

9 $6^2 =$ 36

10 2695, [2702], 2709, 2716

11 $-9 + 12 =$ 3

12 $\frac{1}{3} = 0{\cdot}$[33] $=$ [33]%

13 $(6 \times 8) - 10 =$ 38

14 $90 \div 6 =$ 15

15 25% of 40 = 10

Draw 3 different shapes with a perimeter of 114 cm.

B

1 Write 22 300 in words.
twenty two thousand three hundred

2 Round 20 261 to the nearest 1000. 20 000

3 What value has the 6 in 60 409?
60 thousands or 60 000

4 Is the answer to 289 + 763 nearer 1000 or 1100? 1100

5 Give two factors of 12.
any two from 1, 2, 3, 4, 6 or 12

6 Frances made a model using 60 cubes. 10% are white. How many is this? 6

7 Name a prime number between 15 and 20.
17 or 19

8 $2^3 + 6 =$ 14

9 Ahmed mixes 425 g of flour with 290 g of margarine.
What is the weight of the mixture? 715 g

10 There are 12 pencils in a box.
How many pencils in 4 boxes? 48

11 I spend £6·37 and pay with a £10 note.
How much is my change? £3·63

12 Put these decimals in order, smallest first:
3·37, 3·73, 3·7 3·37, 3·7, 3·73

13 Is an angle of 78° acute or obtuse? acute

14 Emma has 49 bananas.
If she shared them between 8 children, how many would they have each? 6 r 1

15 Chocolate bars cost 45p each.
How many can Desmond buy for £2·25? 5

C

1. $7 \times 7 =$ 49

2. 6020, [6019], 6018, 6017

3. $97 - 32 - 24 =$ 41

4. $537 - 126 =$ 411

5. [8] $\times 14 = 112$

6. $72 \div$ [8] $= 9$

7. $34 + 45 =$ 79

8. $\frac{1}{3} - \frac{1}{4} =$ $\frac{1}{12}$

9. $7^2 + 8 =$ 57

10. 6258, 6251, [6244], 6237

11. $-7 + 4 + 1 =$ -2

12. $\frac{10}{2} =$ 5

13. $(5 \times 7) + 9 =$ 44

14. $135 \div 9 =$ 15

15. $\frac{4}{5}$ of $30 =$ 24

Copy and complete the Function Machine

$\times 6 - 4$

in	out
9	50
12	68
16	92
24	140
8	44
15	86
21	122
32	188
47	278

D

1. Write twenty-seven thousand six hundred and ninety-four in numerals. 27 694

2. 3 units + 22 thousand + 3 hundreds + 2 tens = 22 323

3. Put these numbers in order, largest first: 16 207, 17 206, 12 706   17 206, 16 207, 12 706

4. Estimate the answer to 19×9. 171

5. The temperature is 4°C. Overnight it drops 3 degrees. What is the new temperature? 1°C

6. What are the next two multiples of 6? 72, 78, [84], [90]

7. What is the volume of a cube with sides measuring 5 cm? 125 cm^3

8. What number multiplied by itself gives 100? 10

9. Over a weekend a shop sells 256 packets of crisps. If the original stock was 528, how many packets are left? 272

10. Mr Jones uses 12 tea bags every day. How long will a box of 144 tea bags last? 12 days

11. Complete the ratio, 1:9, 7:[63]

12. I buy 3 cakes at £1·20 each. How much change do I get from £10? £6·40

13. What is this shape?

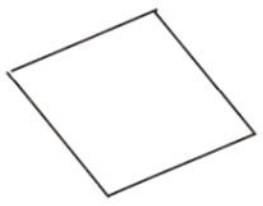

a rhombus

14. Is a kilogram heavier or lighter than a pound? heavier

15. There are three cubes in a box. Two are yellow and one is orange. What chance do I have of pulling out an orange cube? 1 in 3 or $\frac{1}{3}$

Exercise 4

A

1 $8 \times 3 =$ 24

2 5108, 5109, [5110], 5111

3 $42 + 16 + 31 =$ 89

4 $521 + 238 =$ 759

5 $12 \times 8 =$ 96

6 $35 -$ [11] $= 24$

7 $49 \div 7 =$ 7

8 $\frac{1}{2} + \frac{3}{4} =$ $1\frac{1}{4}$

9 $9^2 =$ 81

10 5682, 5694, [5706], 5718

11 $-4 + 8 =$ 4

12 $\frac{1}{5} = 0\cdot$[2] $=$ [20]%

13 $(2 \times 7) - 5 =$ 9

14 $72 \div 4 =$ 18

15 50% of 160 = 80

Copy and complete.

+	6·14	5·31	2·01	1·36
3·25	9·39	8·56	5·26	4·61
4·13	10·27	9·44	6·14	5·49
6·8	12·94	12·11	8·81	8·16
9·54	15·68	14·85	11·55	10·9

B

1 Write 31 670 in words.
thirty-one thousand six hundred and seventy

2 Round 23 049 to the nearest 1000. 23 000

3 What value has the 8 in 20 803?
800 or 8 hundreds

4 Is the answer to 808 + 947 nearer 1700 or 1800? 1800

5 Give two factors of 36.
any two from 1, 2, 3, 4, 6, 9, 12, 18 and 36

6 David made a model using 40 cubes. 20% are blue. How many is this? 8

7 Name a prime number between 30 and 35.
31

8 $4^2 - 3 =$ 13

9 Chris mixes 497 ml of coke with 215 ml of lemonade. How many ml of drink does he have now? 712 ml

10 There are 9 plants in each window box. How many plants in 6 boxes? 54

11 I spend £7·13 and pay with a £10 note. How much is my change? £2·87

12 Put these decimals in order, smallest first: 5·9, 5·92, 5·89 5·89, 5·9, 5·92

13 Is an angle of 125° acute or obtuse? obtuse

14 Eric has 58 sweets. If he shared them between 7 children, how many would they have each? 8 r 2

15 If a paintbrush costs 85p, how many can Jimmy buy for £2·55? 3

C

1. $4 \times 9 =$ 36
2. 5012, 5011, 5010, 5009
3. $47 - 12 - 24 =$ 11
4. $359 - 137 =$ 222
5. 5 $\times 17 = 85$
6. $54 \div$ 9 $= 6$
7. $42 + 56 =$ 98
8. $\frac{1}{2} - \frac{1}{5} =$ $\frac{3}{10}$
9. $5^2 + 2 =$ 27
10. 3508, 3499, 3490, 3481
11. $-6 + 2 + 2 =$ -2
12. $\frac{15}{5} =$ 3
13. $(7 \times 6) + 4 =$ 46
14. $54 \div 3 =$ 18
15. $\frac{5}{6}$ of $48 =$ 40

Draw 3 different shapes with an area of $16\,cm^2$

D

1. Write sixty thousand six hundred and sixty in numerals. 60 660
2. 2 hundreds + 13 thousands + 6 units = 13 206
3. Put these numbers in order, smallest first: 17 607, 607, 17 706 607, 17 607, 17 706
4. Estimate the answer to 29×5? 145
5. The temperature is 1°C. Overnight it rises by 3 degrees. What is the new temperature? 4°C
6. What are the next 2 multiples of 11? 121, 132, 143, 154
7. What is the volume of a cube with sides measuring 1 cm? $1\,cm^3$
8. What number multiplied by itself gives 49? 7
9. A child must go to school for 190 days each year. How many days in a year does a child not spend in school? 175
10. At a quiz there are 60 people sitting at tables of 4. How many tables are there? 15
11. Complete the ratio, 1:9 9:81
12. I buy 4 chocolate bars at 60p each. How much change do I get from £10? £7·60
13. What sort of triangle is this? 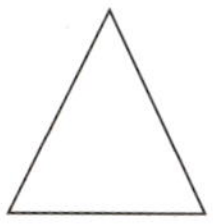 an isoceles triangle
14. Is a gram heavier or lighter than an ounce? lighter
15. There are ten socks in one drawer. 7 are brown and 3 are black. What chance have I got of pulling out a brown sock? 7 in 10 or $\frac{7}{10}$

Exercise 5

A

1 $6 \times 6 =$ 36

2 2199, $\boxed{2200}$, 2201, 2202

3 $21 + 34 + 44 =$ 99

4 $372 + 416 =$ 788

5 $11 \times 6 =$ 66

6 $76 - \boxed{33} = 43$

7 $54 \div 9 =$ 6

8 $\frac{2}{3} + \frac{2}{3} = 1\frac{1}{3}$

9 $2^2 =$ 4

10 7501, $\boxed{7512}$, 7523, 7534

11 $-8 + 15 =$ 7

12 $\frac{3}{4} = 0{\cdot}\boxed{75} = \boxed{75}\%$

13 $(4 \times 9) - 3 =$ 33

14 $68 \div 2 =$ 34

15 25% of 160 = 40

What are the co-ordinates for this shape?

(1,5) (2,5) (3,6) (4,5) (5,5) (4,3) (5,1) (4,1) (3,0) (2,1) (1,1) (2,3)

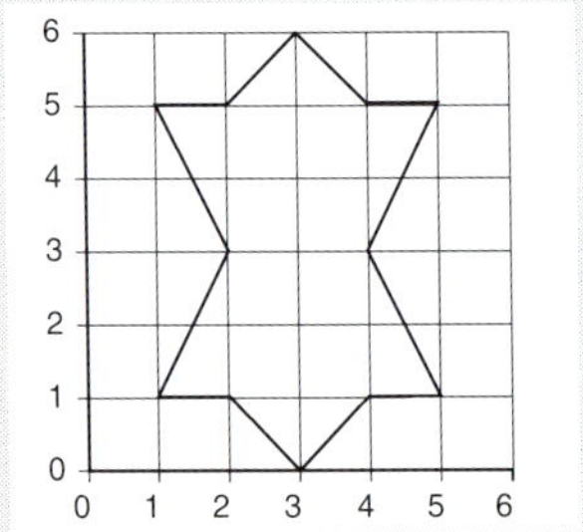

B

1 Write 39 009 in words.
thirty nine thousand and nine

2 Round 29 652 to the nearest 1000. 30 000

3 What value has the 7 in 73 028?
70 000 or 70 thousands

4 Is the answer to 987 + 719 nearer 1600 or 1700? 1700

5 Give two factors of 18.
any two from 1, 2, 3, 6, 9, 18

6 John made a model with 35 bricks.
20% are orange. How many is this? 7

7 Name a prime number between 12 and 18.
13 or 17

8 $3^3 - 7 =$ 20

9 A family travel 527 km on the first day of their holiday.
On the second day they travel 490 km.
How far have they travelled in total? 1017 km

10 There are 6 videos in a pack.
How many videos in 6 packs? 36

11 I spend £8·79, and pay with a £10 note.
How much is my change? £1·21

12 Put these decimals in order, smallest first:
12·12, 12·2, 12·1 12·1, 12·12, 12·2

13 Is an angle of 26° acute or obtuse? acute

14 Ishmail has 70 nuts.
If he shared them between 9 friends, how many would they have each? 7 r 7

15 A hot dog costs 85p.
How many can Lina buy with £4·25? 5

C

1 $6 \times 1 =$ 6

2 3287, 3286, 3285, [3284]

3 $59 - 21 - 16 =$ 22

4 $638 - 406 =$ 232

5 [9] $\times 12 = 108$

6 $49 \div$ [7] $= 7$

7 $65 + 23 =$ 88

8 $\frac{1}{4} - \frac{1}{8} =$ $\frac{1}{8}$

9 $8^2 + 9 =$ 73

10 5217, 5209, 5201, [5193]

11 $-8 + 4 + 1 =$ -3

12 $\frac{12}{3} =$ 4

13 $(6 \times 3) + 5 =$ 23

14 $56 \div 4 =$ 14

15 $\frac{2}{5}$ of $35 =$ 14

Can you make 210 using + and × and all five numbers only once?

2	5
3	19
	17

$(2 \times 19) \times 5 + 3 + 17 = 210$

D

1 Write forty-nine thousand eight hundred in numerals. 49 800

2 4 hundreds + 2 tens + 15 thousands + 3 units = 15 423

3 Put these numbers in order, smallest first: 16 409, 19 604, 1908 1908, 16 409, 19 604

4 Estimate the answer to 29×7. 203

5 The temperature is 5°C. Overnight it rises by 7 degrees. What is the new temperature? 12°C

6 What are the next 2 multiples of 8? 88, 96, [104], [112]

7 What is the volume of a cube with sides measuring 4 cm? 64 cm^3

8 What number multiplied by itself gives 25? 5

9 I record a programme that lasts for 145 minutes. How many minutes are left on a 240 minute tape? 95 minutes

10 108 people attend a concert. They are seated in rows of 6 people. How many rows are there? 18

11 Complete the ratio, 1:11, 10:[110]

12 I buy 5 packets of biscuits at 25p each. How much change do I get from £10? £8·75

13 What is this shape?

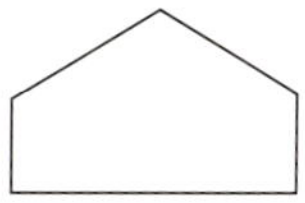

pentagon

14 Is a centimetre longer or shorter than an inch? shorter

15 There are 3 apples in a bag. 2 are red and 1 is green. What chance have I got of pulling out a red one? 2 in 3 or $\frac{2}{3}$

Exercise 6

A

1 $5 \times 8 =$ 40

2 9396, 9397, 9398, [9399]

3 $11 + 56 + 32 =$ 99

4 $254 + 403 =$ 657

5 $11 \times 8 =$ 88

6 $87 -$ [35] $= 52$

7 $72 \div 8 =$ 9

8 $\frac{3}{8} + \frac{1}{4} = \frac{5}{8}$

9 $5^2 =$ 25

10 6354, 6368, 6382, [6396]

11 $-3 + 14 =$ 11

12 $\frac{2}{5} = 0\cdot$[4] $=$ [40]%

13 $(8 \times 7) - 9 =$ 47

14 $119 \div 7 =$ 17

15 25% of 200 = 50

B

1 Write 42 308 in words.
forty-two thousand three hundred and eight

2 Round 40 036 to the nearest 1000. 40 000

3 What value has the 9 in 29 047?
9000 or 9 thousands

4 Is the answer to 759 + 687 nearer 1300 or 1400? 1400

5 Give two factors of 30.
any two from 1, 2, 3, 5, 6, 10, 14, 30

6 Zoë made a model with 48 bricks.
25% are blue. How many is this? 12

7 Name a prime number between 18 and 25.
19 or 23

8 $5^2 + 12 =$ 37

9 Mum buys a vase for £9·95 and a bunch of flowers for £3·80.
How much does she spend in total? £13·75

10 The school caretaker stacks chairs in piles of 7.
How many chairs in 8 piles? 56

11 I spend £18·76, and pay with a £20 note.
How much is my change? £1·24

12 Put these decimals in order, smallest first:
16·82, 16·28, 16·3 16·28, 16·3, 16·82

13 Is an angle of 179° acute or obtuse? obtuse

14 Nicky has 84 flowerpots.
If she shared them between 8 friends, how many would they have each? 10 r 4

15 A child's bus fare is 55p.
How many children can be paid for with £2·75? 5

Draw 3 different shapes with a perimeter of 20 cm.

C

1 $8 \times 8 =$ 64

2 7410, 7409, 7408, 7407

3 $86 - 42 - 23 =$ 21

4 $955 - 534 =$ 421

5 9 $\times 15 = 135$

6 $48 \div$ 8 $= 6$

7 $83 + 16 =$ 99

8 $\frac{2}{3} - \frac{1}{4} =$ $\frac{5}{12}$

9 $6^2 + 4 =$ 40

10 8010, 8004, 7998, 7992

11 $-9 + 3 + 4 =$ -2

12 $\frac{20}{4} =$ 5

13 $(8 \times 4) + 6 =$ 38

14 $120 \div 8 =$ 15

15 $\frac{1}{4}$ of $44 =$ 11

Copy and complete the Function Machine

-16

in	out
59	43
28	12
73	57
41	25
22	6
91	75
107	91
235	219
348	332

D

1 Write thirty-nine thousand and fifty-six in numerals. 39 056

2 7 units + 18 thousands = 18 007

3 Put these numbers in order, largest first: 27 609, 26 907, 27 906. 27 906, 27 609, 26 907

4 Estimate the answer to 8×39. 312

5 The temperature is 7°C. Overnight it drops 2 degrees. What is the new temperature? 5°C

6 What are the next 2 multiples of 12? 120, 132, 144, 156

7 What is the volume of a cube with sides measuring 6 cm? 216 cm^3

8 What number multiplied by itself gives 121? 11

9 The book that Mrs Stewart is reading has 712 pages. She has already read 584 pages. How many pages are left to read? 128

10 Mr Phillips has made 45 buns. He has 1 baking tray, which holds 15 buns. How many times did he have to use the tin? 3 times

11 Complete the ratio, 1:8, 13: 104

12 I buy 2 boxes of cornflakes at £2·75 each. How much change do I get from £10? £4·50

13 What is this shape?

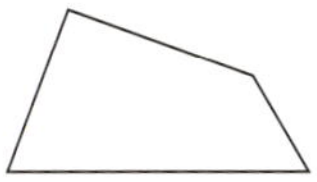

quadrilateral

14 Is a decimetre (10 cm) longer or shorter than a foot? shorter

15 There are 4 coins in a bag. 2 are 10p, 1 is a 5p and 1 is a 2p. What chance have I got of taking out a 10p? 1 in 2 or evens

Exercise 7

A

1 $9 \times 7 =$ 63

2 7409, 7410, [7411], 7412

3 $24 + 34 + 41 =$ 99

4 $625 + 234 =$ 859

5 $11 \times 9 =$ 99

6 $98 -$ [63] $= 35$

7 $27 \div 3 =$ 9

8 $\frac{2}{5} + \frac{4}{5} = 1\frac{1}{5}$

9 $8^2 =$ 64

10 8988, [9003], 9018, 9033

11 $-7 + 20 =$ 13

12 $\frac{1}{10} = 0 \cdot$ [1] $=$ [10]%

13 $(5 \times 3) - 4 =$ 11

14 $57 \div 3 =$ 19

15 50% of 140 = 70

Copy and complete.

×	36	45	29	71
9	324	405	261	639
8	288	360	232	568
6	216	270	174	426
4	144	180	116	284

B

1 Write 48 387 in words.
forty-eight thousand three hundred and eighty-seven

2 Round 49 207 to the nearest 1000. 49 000

3 What value has the 8 in 28 476?
8000 or 8 thousands

4 Is the answer to 826 + 987 nearer 1700 or 1800? 1800

5 Give two factors of 16.
any two from 1, 2, 4, 8 and 16

6 Fiona builds a model with 72 bricks.
25% are red. How many is this? 18

7 Name a prime number between 21 and 30.
23 or 29

8 $6^2 - 8 =$ 28

9 The greengrocer sells 129 kg of black grapes and 293 kg of white grapes.
How many kg of grapes does he sell altogether? 422 kg

10 There are 12 eggs in a dozen.
How many eggs in five dozen? 60

11 I spend £17·62, and pay with a £20 note.
How much is my change? £2·38

12 Put these decimals in order, smallest first:
20·02, 20·20, 20·12 20·02, 20·12, 20·20

13 Is an angle of 89° acute or obtuse? acute

14 Amanda has 78 marbles.
If she shared them between 8 friends, how many would they have each? 9 r 6

15 Pens cost 72p each.
How many can Andrew buy if he has £3·60?
5

C

1 $4 \times 8 = $ 32

2 8340, 8339, 8338, 8337

3 $77 - 32 - 24 = $ 21

4 $748 - 524 = $ 224

5 $\boxed{8} \times 16 = 128$

6 $64 \div \boxed{8} = 8$

7 $74 + 13 = $ 87

8 $\frac{2}{3} - \frac{1}{2} = \frac{1}{6}$

9 $9^2 + 5 = $ 86

10 7421, 7412, 7403, 7394

11 $-7 + 3 + 2 = -2$

12 $\frac{12}{2} = 6$

13 $(2 \times 7) + 5 = $ 19

14 $96 \div 6 = $ 16

15 $\frac{3}{5}$ of $45 = $ 27

Draw 3 different shapes with an area of 24 cm^2.

D

1 Write seventy-nine thousand four hundred and six in numerals. 79 406

2 4 tens + 3 units + 14 thousands = 14 043

3 Put these numbers in order, smallest first: 14 732, 12 742, 12 744 12 742, 12 744, 14 732

4 Estimate the answer to 48×6. 288

5 The temperature is –7°C. Overnight the temperature rises by 5 degrees. What is the new temperature? –2°C

6 What are the next two multiples of 9? 90, 99, 108, 117

7 What is the volume of a cube with sides measuring 10 cm? 1000 cm^3

8 What number multiplied by itself gives 36? 6

9 There are 433 children in the school. 289 school dinners have been ordered. How many children are not having dinners? 144

10 At a netball tournament, 128 children are taking part. The teams each have 8 players, including a reserve. How many teams are taking part? 16

11 Complete the ratio, 1:13, 4:52

12 I buy 4 bottles of lemonade at £1·10 each. How much change do I get from £10? £5·60

13 What is this shape?

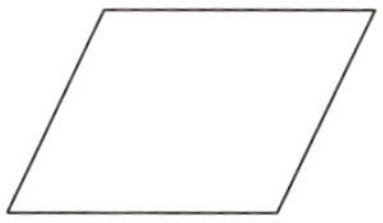

a parallelogram

14 Is a foot longer or shorter than a metre? shorter

15 Sarah is in a race with 3 other people. What chance does she have of winning? 1 in 4 or $\frac{1}{4}$

Exercise 8

A

1 $7 \times 5 =$ 35

2 [8449], 8450, 8451, 8452

3 $26 + 32 + 53 =$ 111

4 $754 + 205 =$ 959

5 $12 \times 10 =$ 120

6 $67 -$ [43] $= 24$

7 $36 \div 6 =$ 6

8 $\frac{1}{3} + \frac{4}{6} =$ 1

9 $7^2 =$ 49

10 9462, 9474, 9786, [9798]

11 $-7 + 16 =$ 9

12 $\frac{3}{5} = 0 \cdot$ [6] $=$ [60]%

13 $(6 \times 2) - 8 =$ 4

14 $126 \div 9 =$ 14

15 25% of 80 = 20

What are the co-ordinates for this shape?

(–5,6) (–4,6) (–3,5) (–2,6) (–1,6) (–2,4) (–1,2) (–2,0) (–3,2) (–4,0) (–5,2) (–4,4)

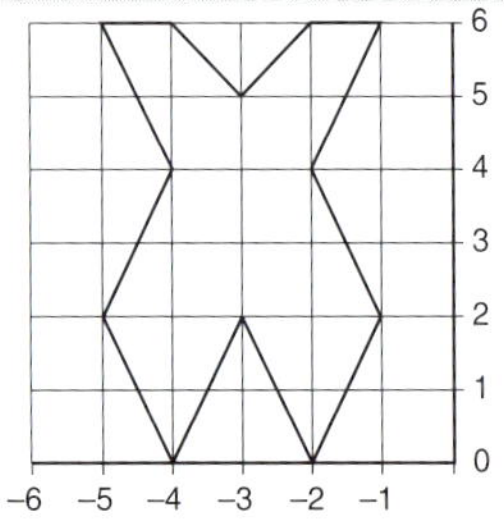

B

1 Write 89 400 in words.
eighty-nine thousand four hundred

2 Round 99 608 to the nearest 1000. 100 000

3 What value has the 6 in 68 982?
60 000 or 60 thousands

4 Is the answer to 657 + 875 nearer 1500 or 1600? 1500

5 Give two factors of 48.
any two of 1, 2, 3, 4, 6, 8, 12, 16, 24 and 48

6 Frank makes a model with 56 cubes. 25% are orange. How many is this? 14

7 Name a prime number between 25 and 34.
29 or 31

8 $8^2 + 16 =$ 80

9 There are 376 pupils in the infant school and 451 in the junior school. How many pupils altogether? 827

10 In assembly, 9 children sit in each row. How many children are there in 8 rows? 72

11 I spend £15·08, and pay with a £20 note. How much is my change? £4·92

12 Put these decimals in order, smallest first: 27·27, 27·2, 27·72 27·2, 27·27, 27·72

13 Is an angle of 78° acute or obtuse? obtuse

14 Victoria has 58 stamps. If she shared them between 7 friends, how many would they have each? 8 r 2

15 A bag of popcorn costs 67p. How many can I buy with £3·35? 5

C

1. $9 \times 5 =$ 45
2. 2705, 2704, 2703, [2702]
3. $98 - 36 - 21 =$ 41
4. $866 - 425 =$ 441
5. [9] $\times 16 = 144$
6. $63 \div$ [9] $= 7$
7. $72 + 24 =$ 96
8. $\frac{4}{5} - \frac{1}{10} = \frac{7}{10}$
9. $4^2 + 10 =$ 26
10. [4357], 4351, 4345, 4339
11. $-6 + 0 + 4 =$ −2
12. $\frac{30}{5} =$ 6
13. $(8 \times 8) + 2 =$ 66
14. $76 \div 4 =$ 19
15. $\frac{1}{5}$ of $60 =$ 12

Can you make 284 using – and × and these five numbers only once?

7, 6, 24, 4, 17

$(17 \times 6) - 7 - 24 \times 4$

D

1. Write eighty-three thousand two hundred and nine in numerals. 83 209
2. 3 units + 18 thousands = 18 003
3. Put these numbers in order, largest first: 7676, 767, 7767 7767, 7676, 767
4. Estimate the answer to 52×7. 364
5. The temperature is –4°C. Overnight it rises by 4 degrees. What is the new temperature? 0°C
6. What are the next two multiples of 7? 98, 105, [112], [119]
7. What is the volume of a cube with sides measuring 7 cm? 343 cm^3
8. What number multiplied by itself gives 144? 12
9. In a survey of 776 people, 487 said their favourite TV programme was 'Coronation Street'. How many people had a different favourite? 289
10. Lucy's dad ordered cans of lemonade from the supermarket. He ordered 75 cans in packs of 15. How many packs were there? 5
11. Complete the ratio, 12:4, 3:[1]
12. I buy 2 tickets for the cinema at £3·25 each. How much change do I get from £10? £3·50
13. What is this shape?

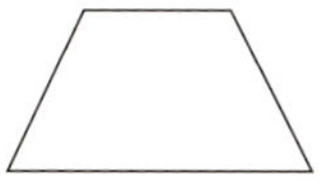

a trapezium

14. Is a mile longer or shorter than 1 km? longer
15. There are 8 sweets in a packet. There are the same number of strawberry, lemon, lime and orange. What chance have I got of getting a lemon one? 2 in 8 or 1 in 4

Exercise 9

A

1 $8 \times 6 =$ 48

2 4379, [4380], 4381, 4382

3 $31 + 42 + 56 =$ 129

4 $428 + 342 =$ 770

5 $11 \times 10 =$ 110

6 $46 -$ [35] $= 11$

7 $32 \div 4 =$ 8

8 $\frac{1}{4} + \frac{1}{4} = \frac{1}{2}$

9 $1^2 = 1$

10 3002, [3020], 3038, 3056

11 $-5 + 30 =$ 25

12 $\frac{2}{3} = 0{\cdot}$[66] $=$ [66]%

13 $(4 \times 3) - 6 =$ 6

14 $104 \div 8 =$ 13

15 50% of 90 = 45

Draw 3 different shapes with a perimeter of 16 cm.

B

1 Write 96 908 in words.
ninety-six thousand nine hundred and eight

2 Round 108 207 to the nearest 1000. 108 000

3 What value has the 7 in 117 681?
7000 or 7 thousands

4 Is the answer to 816 + 887 nearer 1600 or 1700? 1700

5 Give 2 factors of 72.
any two of 1, 2, 3, 4, 6, 8, 9, 12, 18, 24, 36 and 72

6 Sheila builds a model with 84 bricks. 25% are green. How many is this? 21

7 Name a prime number between 32 and 45.
37 or 41 or 43

8 $11^2 + 6 =$ 127

9 The fabric shop sold 212 m of striped fabric and 696 m of plain fabric in one week. How much was sold altogether? 908 m

10 The teacher puts 7 paintings on each display board. She uses 7 display boards altogether. How many paintings does she display? 49

11 I spend £13·13, and pay with a £20 note. How much is my change? £6·87

12 Put these decimals in order, smallest first:
36·17, 36·7, 36·71 same order

13 Is an angle of 31° acute or obtuse? acute

14 Natalie has 150 pencils.
If she shared them between 12 friends, how many would they have each? 12 r 6

15 Yo-yos are 57p each. How many can I buy for £4·56? 8

C

1 $7 \times 8 =$ 56

2 9741, 9740, [9739], 9738

3 $69 - 13 - 35 =$ 21

4 $457 - 236 =$ 221

5 [8] $\times 19 = 152$

6 $24 \div$ [4] $= 6$

7 $21 + 75 =$ 96

8 $\frac{5}{6} - \frac{1}{3} =$ $\frac{5}{6}$ or $\frac{1}{2}$

9 $7^2 + 7 =$ 56

10 [2609], 2601, 2593, 2585

11 $-8 + 3 + 4 =$ −1

12 $\frac{24}{6} =$ 4

13 $(4 \times 4) + 3 =$ 19

14 $108 \div 6 =$ 18

15 $\frac{2}{7}$ of $42 =$ 12

Copy and complete the Function Machine

÷8

in	out
72	9
96	12
120	15
112	14
144	18
168	21
200	25
240	30
328	41

D

1 Write forty thousand and eight in numerals.
40 008

2 17 thousands + 2 units + 2 tens = 17 022

3 Put these numbers in order, smallest first:
12 912, 91 212, 21 912 12 912, 21 912, 91 212

4 Estimate the answer to 9×61. 549

5 The temperature is −8°C. Overnight it rises by 3 degrees.
What is the new temperature? −5°C

6 What are the next two multiples of 8?
104, 112, [120], [128]

7 What is the volume of a cube with sides measuring 9 cm? 729 cm^3

8 What number multiplied by itself gives 16? 4

9 846 spectators are watching a football match. If 688 support team A, how many spectators support team B? 158

10 A farmer planted 120 new trees in rows of 15. How many rows are there? 8

11 Complete the ratio, 1:15 5:[75]

12 I buy 3 plants at £1·75 each. How much change do I get from 10? £4·75

13 What is this shape?

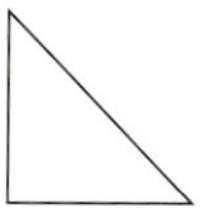

right-angled triangle

14 Is a kilogram heavier or lighter than a stone?
lighter

15 What chance have I got of getting an even number if I throw a 1–6 dice? 1 in 2 or evens

Exercise 10

A

1 $3 \times 9 =$ 27

2 5008, 5009, 5010, 5011

3 $86 + 21 + 43 =$ 150

4 $555 + 244 =$ 799

5 $12 \times 5 =$ 60

6 $58 -$ 34 $= 24$

7 $21 \div 7 =$ 3

8 $\frac{1}{2} + \frac{1}{6} = \frac{4}{6}$ or $\frac{2}{3}$

9 $10^2 =$ 100

10 8257, 8274, 8291, 8308

11 $-8 + 16 =$ 8

12 $\frac{4}{5} = 0{\cdot}$ 8 $=$ 80 %

13 $(6 \times 7) - 9 =$ 33

14 $102 \div 6 =$ 17

15 50% of $270 =$ 135

Copy and complete.

×	3·21	4·78	9·01	5·73
7	22·47	33·46	63·07	40·11
9	28·89	43·02	81·09	51·57
5	16·05	23·9	45·05	28·65
8	25·68	38·24	72·08	45·84

B

1 Write 99 999 in words.
ninety-nine thousand nine hundred and ninety-nine

2 Round 119 862 to the nearest 1000. 120 000

3 What value has the 1 in 123 456?
100 000 or 100 thousands

4 Is the answer to 587 + 768 nearer 1300 or 1400? 1400

5 Give two factors of 64.
any two of 1, 2, 4, 8, 16, 32, 64

6 Stefan builds a model with 120 cubes. 10% are black. How many is this? 12

7 Name a prime number between 42 and 56.
43 or 47 or 53

8 $12^2 + 16 =$ 160

9 In a survey, 1326 children said the Big Wheel was their favourite funfair ride. 272 preferred the Dodgems. How many children were surveyed? 1598

10 Wanda puts 6 apples in each bag. How many apples will go into 8 bags? 48

11 I spend £11·62, and pay with a £20 note. How much is my change? £8·38

12 Put these decimals in order, smallest first: 106·47, 106·74, 106·40 106·40, 106·47, 106·74

13 Is an angle of 143° acute or obtuse? obtuse

14 Jimmy has 112 stickers. If she shared them between 11 children, how many would they have each? 10 r 1

15 Ice-lollies are 87p each. How many can be bought for £4·35? 5

C

1. $9 \times 9 =$ 81
2. 5639, 5638, 5637, 5636
3. $79 - 42 - 17 =$ 20
4. $528 - 416 =$ 112
5. $7 \times 18 = 126$
6. $40 \div 5 = 8$
7. $37 + 43 =$ 80
8. $\frac{3}{5} - \frac{1}{10} =$ $\frac{5}{10}$ or $\frac{1}{2}$
9. $4^2 + 3 =$ 19
10. 6003, 5997, 5991, 5985
11. $-9 + 5 + 4 =$ 0
12. $\frac{56}{8} =$ 7
13. $(9 \times 5) + 3 =$ 48
14. $98 \div 7 =$ 14
15. $\frac{3}{8}$ of 56 = 21

Draw 3 different shapes with an area of 32 cm².

D

1. Write ninety-eight thousand eight hundred and seven in numerals. 98 807
2. 8 tens + 3 units + 19 thousands + 4 hundreds = 19 483
3. Put these numbers in order, largest first: 27 297, 29 729, 7920 29 729, 27 297, 7920
4. Estimate the answer to 4×91 to the nearest ten. 360
5. The temperature is –7°C. Overnight it drops another 3 degrees.
   What is the new temperature? –10°C
6. What are the next 2 multiples of 11? 176, 187, 198, 209
7. What is the volume of a cube with sides measuring 8 cm? 512 cm³
8. What number multiplied by itself gives 49? 7
9. There are 972 cars in a 2-storey car park.
   If there are 587 cars on the first floor,
   how many are parked on the second floor? 385
10. 72 children go on a school trip.
    4 children sleep in each room.
    How many rooms are needed? 18
11. Complete the ratio, 1:18 3:54
12. I buy 3 books at £2·45 each. How much change do I get from £10? £2·65
13. What is this shape? 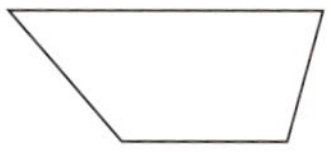 quadrilateral
14. Is a gallon more or less than a litre? more
15. In my purse there are three 20p pieces, two 2p pieces and one 1p piece. What is the chance of my taking out a bronze coin? 1 in 2 or evens

Exercise 11

A

1 $5 \times$ [7] $= 35$

2 23 475, 23 476, 23 477, [23 478]

3 $56 + 22 + 15 =$ 93

4 $423 + 128 =$ 551

5 $14 \times 5 =$ 70

6 $72 -$ [35] $= 37$

7 $19 \div 3 = 5$ r [4]

8 $1\frac{2}{3} + \frac{2}{3} = 2\frac{1}{3}$

9 $2^3 = 8$

10 47 371, 47 380, 47 389, [47 398]

11 $0{\cdot}75 = \frac{3}{4} =$ [75]%

12 $-12 + 6 =$ −6

13 $(7 \times 8) - 16 =$ 40

14 $52 \div 3 = 17$ r [1]

15 $1{\cdot}3 + 2{\cdot}9 =$ 4·2

B

1 Write 38·6 in words. thirty-eight point six

2 What value has the 6 in 26·73? 6 units

3 What is the product of 8 and 9? 72

4 How many times does 16 go into 50? 3 r 2

5 $23 \div 10 =$ 2·3

6 $4200 \div 60 =$ 70

7 Is 16 a factor of 48? yes

8 Write 1·00 am using the 24 hour clock. 13·00

9 385 people attended a school concert on Monday and 397 people on Tuesday. How many attended altogether? 782

10 During the school holidays, Joe watches TV for 4 hours each day. How many hours is this a fortnight? 56

11 (2^2) to power of three = 64

12 Does this net make a cube?

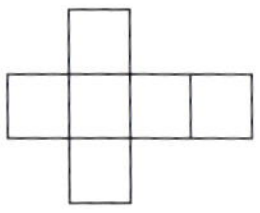

yes

13 What is the perimeter of a rectangle measuring 6 cm x 3 cm? 18 cm

14 Increase £10 by 50%. £15

15 Two of the angles in a triangle equal 90°. What is the third angle? 90°

What are the co-ordinates for this shape?

(−6,1) (−5,3) (−6,5) (−5,6) (−4,5) (−3,6) (−2,5) (−1,6) (0,5) (−1,3) (0,1) (−2,0) (−3,3) (−4,1)

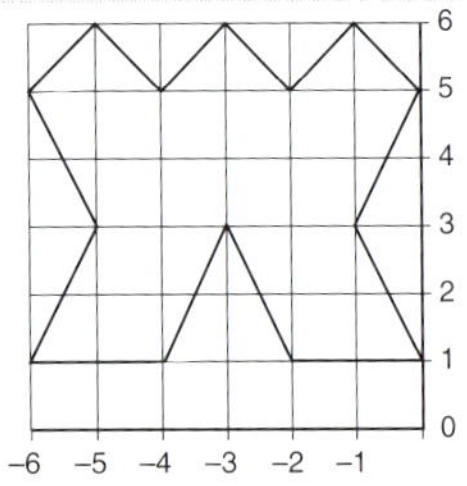

C

1 $\boxed{6} \times 3 = 18$

2 43 110, $\boxed{43\,109}$, 43 108, 43 107

3 $76 - 47 = 29$

4 $456 - 138 = 318$

5 $23 \times 2 = 46$

6 $26 \div 4 = \boxed{6}$ r 2

7 $38 + 47 = 85$

8 $1\frac{2}{5} - \frac{3}{10} = 1\frac{1}{10}$

9 $4^2 - 9 = 7$

10 54 274, 54 264, 54 254, $\boxed{54\,244}$

11 $-12 + 4 - 6 = -14$

12 $\frac{3}{12} = \frac{\boxed{1}}{4}$

13 $(4 \times 9) + 18 = 54$

14 $37 \div 2 = \boxed{18}$ r 1

15 40% of 90 = 36

Can you make 92 using – and × and all five numbers only once.

3	4
26	7
	32

$(32 \times 4) - 26 - 7 - 3 = 92$

D

1 Write thirty-eight point seven in numerals. 38·7

2 15 thousands + 2 units + 4 hundreds = 15 402

3 Round 2·75 to the nearest whole number. 3

4 $0{\cdot}2 \times 10 = 2$

5 Continue the pattern: 21, 15, 11, $\boxed{5}$, $\boxed{-1}$

6 $2100 \times 40 = 84\,000$

7 Is 98 a multiple of 7? yes

8 What is the volume of a cuboid with sides measuring 1 cm, 2 cm and 3 cm? 6 cm^3

9 By midday the Wilson family had travelled 362 km. The total distance, to be travelled was 1290 km.
How many km had they still to go? 928 km

10 Jane has 60 pencils.They are in packs of 15. How many packs has she got? 4

11 Complete the ratio, 12:36 1:$\boxed{3}$

12 I buy 3 boxes of chocolate which cost £3·50 each. How much change will I get from £20? £9·50

13 What is the area of a shape measuring 8 cm by 4 cm? 32 cm^2

14 The scores in a test were: 63, 72, 63, 65, 70, 63. What is the mode? 63

15 5 phone calls are made. 3 calls are made by men and 2 by women.
What is the probability of a caller being a man? 3 in 5 or $\frac{3}{5}$

Exercise 12

A

1 $6 \times \boxed{7} = 42$

2 42 167, 42 168, 42 169, $\boxed{42\,170}$

3 $35 + 24 + 36 = 95$

4 $267 + 315 = 582$

5 $15 \times 7 = 105$

6 $61 - \boxed{25} = 36$

7 $27 \div 4 = 6 \text{ r } \boxed{3}$

8 $2\frac{1}{4} + \frac{1}{4} = 2\frac{1}{2}$

9 $3^3 = 27$

10 61 543, $\boxed{61\,555}$, 61 567, 61 579

11 $0{\cdot}5 = \frac{1}{2} = \boxed{50}\%$

12 $-10 + 5 = -5$

13 $(6 \times 3) - 12 = 6$

14 $62 \div 4 = 15 \text{ r } \boxed{2}$

15 $2{\cdot}5 + 4{\cdot}6 = 7{\cdot}1$

Draw 3 different shapes with a perimeter of 18 cm.

B

1 Write 1634 in words.
one hundred and sixty-three point four

2 What value has the 8 in 8374?
8 thousands or 8000

3 What is the product of 12 and 10? 120

4 Estimate how many times does 8 go into 90?
11 r 2

5 $67 \div 10 = 6{\cdot}7$

6 $6300 \div 90 = 70$

7 Is 18 a factor of 48? no

8 Write 3·15 pm using the 24 hour clock. 15·15

9 During the first hour of a telephone competition, 937 people rang. 849 people telephoned in the second hour. How many people rang altogether? 1786

10 Every week Susan saves £3. How much will she have saved after 26 weeks? £78

11 $(3^2)^2 = 81$

12 Does this net make a cube?

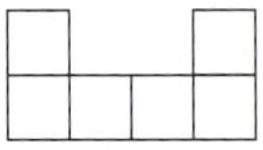

no

13 What is the perimeter of a rectangle measuring 4 cm x 5 cm? 18 cm

14 Increase £10 by 25%. £12·50

15 Two of the angles in a triangle equal 120°. What is the third angle? 60°

C

1. $\boxed{7} \times 4 = 28$
2. 37 002, 37 001, 37 000, $\boxed{36\,999}$
3. $26 - 17 =$ 9
4. $348 - 219 =$ 129
5. $48 \times 7 =$ 336
6. $13 \div 3 = \boxed{4}$ r 1
7. $58 + 38 =$ 96
8. $5\frac{2}{3} - \frac{1}{3} = 5\frac{1}{3}$
9. $9^2 - 7 =$ 74
10. 87 301, 87 201, 87 101, $\boxed{87\,001}$
11. $-15 + 8 - 6 =$ –13
12. $\frac{15}{36} = \frac{\boxed{5}}{12}$
13. $(7 \times 8) + 13 =$ 69
14. $59 \div 4 = \boxed{14}$ r $\boxed{3}$
15. 70% of 60 = 42

Copy and complete the Function Machine

$\times 7 + 2$

in	out
8	58
12	86
13	93
18	128
22	156
26	184
35	247
41	289
52	366

D

1. Write forty-nine point one in numerals. 49·1
2. 2 units + 17 thousands + 8 tens = 17 082
3. Round 1·8 to the nearest whole number. 2
4. $0{\cdot}7 \times 10 =$ 7
5. Continue the pattern: 17, 10, 3, $\boxed{-4}$, $\boxed{-11}$
6. $2600 \times 50 =$ 130 000
7. Is 85 a multiple of 8? no
8. What is the volume of a cuboid with sides measuring 2 cm, 2 cm and 3 cm? 12 cm^3
9. The newsagent received 2325 newspapers each day. 405 were delivered by the newspaper delivery staff. How many were left to sell in the shop? 1920
10. The children are asked to line up in groups of 12. There are 84 children. How many lines are there? 7
11. Complete the ratio, 7:42 1:$\boxed{6}$
12. I buy 4 cartons of juice at £1·25 each. How much change do I get from £20? £15
13. What is the area of a shape measuring 9 cm by 12cm? 108 cm^2
14. Books have the following number of pages: 107, 109, 107, 110. What is the mode? 107
15. There are 10 toys in a lucky dip. 5 are cars. 5 are dolls. What is the probability of picking a toy car? 1 in 2 or evens

Exercise 13

A

1 $2 \times \boxed{7} = 14$

2 84 298, 84 299, $\boxed{84\,300}$, 84 301

3 $27 + 43 + 19 =$ 89

4 $416 + 257 =$ 673

5 $16 \times 5 =$ 80

6 $53 - \boxed{24} = 29$

7 $47 \div 9 = 5$ r $\boxed{2}$

8 $3\frac{1}{2} + \frac{1}{6} = 3\frac{2}{3}$

9 $4^3 =$ 64

10 42 593, $\boxed{42\,607}$, 42 621, 42 635

11 $0{\cdot}25 = \frac{1}{4} = \boxed{25}\%$

12 $-16 + 7 =$ −9

13 $(5 \times 7) - 19 =$ 16

14 $124 \div 7 = 17$ r $\boxed{5}$

15 $6{\cdot}7 + 1{\cdot}5 =$ 8·2

Copy and complete.

÷	6	4	7	9
24	4	6	3·4	2·66
63	10·5	15·75	9	7
48	8	12	6·8	5·3
126	21	31·5	18	14

B

1 Write 17·95 in words.
one hundred and seventy-nine point five

2 What value has the 3 in 27·93?
three hundredths or $\frac{3}{100}$

3 What is the product of 13 and 3? 39

4 How many times does 16 go into 50? 3 r 2

5 $321 \div 10 =$ 32·1

6 $8100 \div 90 =$ 90

7 Is 12 a factor of 50? no

8 Write 1800 using the 12 hour clock. 6 pm

9 In her stamp collection, Kelly has 684 stamps in one album and 578 stamps in another. How many stamps does she have altogether?
1262

10 If each of the 30 children in orange class is 11 years old, how many years have they been alive altogether? 330 years

11 (1^3) to power of 3 = 1

12 Does this net make a cube?

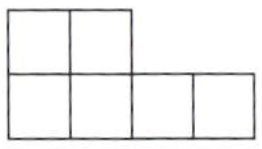

no

13 What is the perimeter of a rectangle measuring 12 m × 1 m? 26 m

14 Increase 20 by 20%. £24

15 Two of the angles in a triangle equal 110°. What is the third angle? 70°

C

1 [8] $\times 5 = 40$

2 79 511, 79 510, [79 509], 79 508

3 $63 - 26 =$ 37

4 $736 - 638 =$ 98

5 $76 \times 9 =$ 684

6 $52 \div 8 =$ [6] r 4

7 $45 + 49 =$ 94

8 $3\frac{4}{5} - \frac{1}{5} =$ $3\frac{3}{5}$

9 $7^2 - 9 =$ 40

10 [95 278], 94 278, 93 278, 92 278

11 $-20 + 6 - 7 =$ -21

12 $\frac{16}{24} = \frac{[4]}{6}$

13 $(6 \times 3) + 15 =$ 33

14 $50 \div 3 =$ [16] r 2

15 80% of 120 = 96

Draw 3 different shapes with an area of 28 cm².

D

1 Write one hundred and seven point nine in numerals. 107·9

2 21 thousands + 6 units = 21 006

3 Round 2·4 to the nearest whole number. 2

4 $0{\cdot}9 \times 10 =$ 9

5 Continue the pattern: 24, 13, 2, [−9], [−20]

6 $2700 \times 30 =$ 81 000

7 Is 89 a multiple of 9? no

8 What is the volume of a cuboid with sides measuring 3 cm, 2 cm and 3 cm? 18 cm³

9 Donald had saved £52·73. He bought a game costing £5·95. How much did he have left? £46·78

10 There are 65 cars in a car park. They are parked in groups of 5. How many groups are there? 13

11 Complete the ratio, 9:54 1:[6]

12 I buy 4 files which cost £1·95 each. How much change do I get from £20? £12·20

13 What is the area of a shape measuring 7 m by 14 m? 98 m²

14 The results at football matches were: 3–2, 1–0, 1–1, 3–2, 2–1, 3–4. What is the mode? 3–2

15 There are 10 shoes under a bed. 2 shoes are brown and 8 shoes are black. What is the probability of finding a brown shoe? 2 in 10 or 1 in 5

Exercise 14

A

1 $8 \times \boxed{7} = 56$

2 89 998, 89 999, [90 000], 90 001

3 $39 + 14 + 33 =$ 86

4 $607 + 248 =$ 855

5 $17 \times 6 =$ 102

6 $64 - \boxed{27} = 37$

7 $41 \div 5 = 8 \text{ r } \boxed{1}$

8 $\frac{1}{6} + 1\frac{2}{3} = 1\frac{5}{6}$

9 $5^3 =$ 125

10 36 875, 36 888, [36 901], 36 914

11 $0{\cdot}125 = \boxed{\frac{1}{8}} = \boxed{12\frac{1}{2}}\ \%$

12 $-14 + 9 = -5$

13 $(8 \times 4) - 27 =$ 5

14 $97 \div 6 = 16 \text{ r } \boxed{1}$

15 $3{\cdot}2 + 2{\cdot}8 =$ 6

What are the co-ordinates for this shape?

(0,–1) (1,–3) (2,–1) (3,–3) (4,–1) (5,–3) (6,–1) (6,–6) (5,–4) (4,–6) (3,–4) (2,–6) (1,–4) (0,–6)

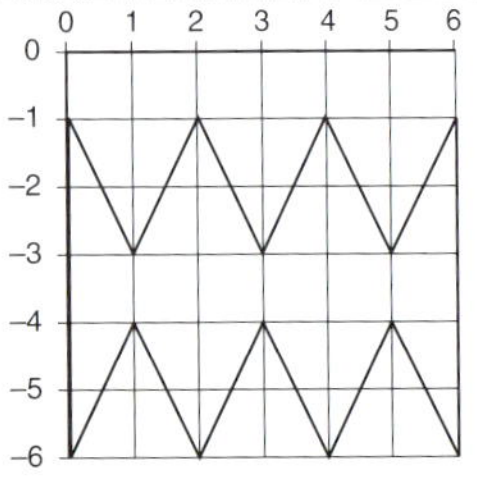

B

1 Write 272.9 in words.
two hundred and seventy-two point nine

2 What value has the 8 in 63·8? 8 tenths or $\frac{8}{10}$

3 What is the product of 15 and 4? 60

4 How many times does 7 go into 100? 14 r 2

5 $821 \div 10 =$ 82·1

6 $5400 \div 60 =$ 90

7 Is 8 a factor of 100? no

8 Write 11·45 am using the 24 hour clock. 11·45

9 Jack and Patrick went out for a meal. Jack's meal cost £3·85 and Patrick's cost £3·95. How much was the bill altogether? £7·80

10 There are 8 classes in the school and each class has 700 building blocks. How many blocks are there in school altogether? 5600

11 $(3^2)^2 =$ 81

12 Does this net make a cube?

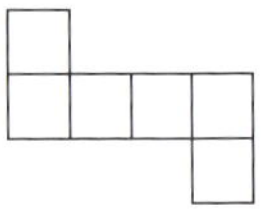

yes

13 What is the perimeter of a rectangle measuring 8 cm × 7 cm? 30 cm

14 Increase £20 by 50%. £30

15 Two of the angles in a triangle equal 135°. What is the third angle? 45°

C

1. [9] × 7 = 63
2. 52 341, 52 340, [52 339], 52 338
3. 83 − 45 = 38
4. 961 − 524 = 437
5. 37 × 6 = 222
6. 87 ÷ 9 = [9] r 6
7. 63 + 28 = 91
8. $4\frac{1}{3} - \frac{2}{3} = 3\frac{2}{3}$
9. $2^2 - 1 = 3$
10. 73 290, 73 190, 73 090, [72 990]
11. −14 + 7 − 9 = −16
12. $\frac{9}{18} = \frac{[1]}{2}$
13. (7 × 5) + 14 = 49
14. 78 ÷ 5 = [15] r 3
15. 40% of 50 = 20

Can you make 118 using + and × and all five numbers only once

9	4
2	37
	48

(37 × 9) × 2 + 4 + 48 = 118

D

1. Write two hundred and sixteen point three in numerals. 216·3
2. 2 tenths + 3 hundreds + 4 tens + 1 unit = 341·2
3. Round 8·14 to the nearest whole number. 8
4. 2·4 × 10 = 24
5. Continue the pattern: 25, 12, −1, [−14], [−27]
6. 2500 × 50= 125 000
7. Is 103 a multiple of 3? no
8. What is the volume of a cuboid with sides measuring 3 cm, 2 cm and 2 cm? 12 cm^3
9. Marie had collected 1009 different stickers. 475 were football stickers. How many stickers were not football ones? 534
10. The plates are stacked in piles of 15. There are 90 plates. How many piles? 6
11. Complete the ratio, 9:81 1:[9]
12. I buy 4 bunches of flowers at £2·25 each. How much change will I get from £20? £11
13. What is the area of a shape measuring 13 cm by 13 cm? 169 cm^2
14. Over a week, the temperatures were 21°C, 20°C, 22°C, 20°C, 21°C, 21°C. What is the mode? 21°C
15. There are 6 sweets in a bag. 4 are strawberry flavour and 2 are lemon flavour. What is the probability of choosing a lemon flavoured sweet? 1 in 3 or $\frac{1}{3}$

Exercise 15

A

1 $4 \times$ [9] $= 36$

2 51 008, 51 009, [51 010], 51 011

3 $67 + 13 + 16 =$ 96

4 $355 + 316 =$ 671

5 $18 \times 7 =$ 126

6 $33 -$ [19] $= 14$

7 $23 \div 7 = 3$ r [2]

8 $2\frac{1}{5} + \frac{2}{10} = 2\frac{2}{5}$

9 $5^4 =$ 625

10 52 351, 52 362, 52 373, [52 384]

11 $0{\cdot}2 =$ [$\frac{1}{5}$] $=$ [20]%

12 $-17 + 10 =$ −7

13 $(7 \times 6) - 25 =$ 17

14 $95 \div 7 = 13$ r [4]

15 $5{\cdot}6 + 1{\cdot}7 =$ 7·3

Draw 3 different shapes with a perimeter of 12 cm.

B

1 Write 1529·7 in words.
one thousand five hundred and twenty-nine point seven

2 What value has the 2 in 312·7? 2 units

3 What is the product of 15 and 7? 105

4 How many times does 9 go into 120? 13 r 3

5 $467 \div 10 =$ 46·7

6 $4800 \div 30 =$ 160

7 Is 12 a factor of 120? yes

8 Write 17·10 using the 12 hour clock. 5·10 pm

9 Josephine has a collection of soft toys. She has 285 teddy-bears and 138 other animals. How many toys altogether? 423

10 A shop sells candles in bundles of 9. On Saturday 20 bundles were sold. How many candles is this? 180

11 $(2^3)^2 =$ 64

12 Does this net make a cube?

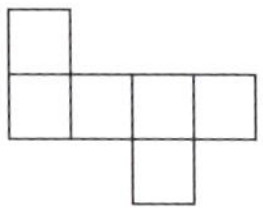

yes

13 What is the perimeter of a rectangle measuring 13 m × 3 m? 32 m

14 Increase £10 by 10%. £11

15 Two of the angles in a triangle equal 115°. What is the third angle? 65°

C

1. $\boxed{4} \times 8 = 32$
2. 98 653, $\boxed{98\,652}$, 98 651, 98 650
3. $42 - 27 =$ 15
4. $834 - 409 =$ 425
5. $65 \times 8 =$ 520
6. $31 \div 7 = \boxed{4}$ r 3
7. $46 + 35 =$ 81
8. $3\frac{1}{2} - \frac{1}{5} = 3\frac{3}{10}$
9. $4^2 - 5 =$ 11
10. $\boxed{33\,000}$, 32 900, 32 800, 32 700
11. $-19 + 3 - 5 =$ −21
12. $\frac{16}{20} = \frac{\boxed{4}}{5}$
13. $(5 \times 9) + 17 =$ 62
14. $93 \div 7 = \boxed{13}$ r 2
15. 60% of 80 = 48

Copy and complete the Function Machine

× 4 − 3

in	out
12	45
25	97
32	125
16	61
18	69
27	105
47	185
53	209
61	241

D

1. Write seven hundred and eight point two three in numerals. 708·23
2. 3 units + 5 tenths + 4 tens + 7 hundreds = 743·5
3. Round 8·6 to the nearest whole number. 9
4. $8{\cdot}5 \times 10 =$ 85
5. Continue the pattern: 20, 11, 2, $\boxed{-7}$, $\boxed{-16}$
6. $1300 \times 50 =$ 65 000
7. Is 128 a multiple of 8? yes
8. What is the volume of a cuboid with sides measuring 5 cm, 2 cm and 5 cm? 50 cm^3
9. Kirsten had £95·61 in her savings account. She withdrew £9·50. How much was left? £86·11
10. Mary has 144 stickers. 12 fit on a page. How many pages can she fill? 12
11. Complete the ratio, 12:120 1:$\boxed{10}$
12. I buy 3 books which cost £3·50 each. How much change do I get from £20? £9·50
13. What is the area of a shape measuring 8 m by 16 m? 128 m^2
14. These are amounts in money boxes: 89p, £1·12, £1·10, £1·12, £1·00. What is the mode? £1·12
15. There are 20 football stickers in a box. 8 are Manchester United stickers. What is the probability of picking a Manchester United sticker? 8 in 20 or 4 in 10

Exercise 16

A

1 $10 \times$ 5 $= 50$

2 49 657, 49 658, 49 659, 49 660

3 $46 + 24 + 22 =$ 92

4 $634 + 238 =$ 872

5 $13 \times 9 =$ 117

6 $82 -$ 44 $= 38$

7 $59 \div 9 = 6$ r 5

8 $\frac{3}{8} + 2\frac{1}{4} = 2\frac{5}{8}$

9 $2^4 =$ 16

10 93 987, 94 001, 94 015, 94 029

11 $0{\cdot}1 = \frac{1}{10} =$ 10%

12 $-15 + 3 =$ −12

13 $(6 \times 6) - 27 =$ 9

14 $115 \div 8 = 14$ r 3

15 $2{\cdot}7 + 3{\cdot}4 =$ 6·1

Copy and complete.

–	5·31	8·03	12·64	9·55
37	31·69	28·97	24·36	27·45
28	22·69	19·97	15·36	18·45
41	35·69	32·97	28·36	31·45
16	10·69	7·97	3·36	6·45

B

1 Write 2043·61 in words.
two thousand and forty-three point six one

2 What value has the 5 in 232·51? 5 tenths or $\frac{5}{10}$

3 What is the product of 15 and 5? 75

4 How many times does 12 go into 100? 8 r 4

5 $31{\cdot}2 \div 10 =$ 3·12

6 $3600 \div 120 =$ 30

7 Is 17 a factor of 70? no

8 Write 12·25 am using the 24 hour clock. 00·25

9 712 people live in one block of flats and 859 live in the neighbouring block. How many people altogether? 1571

10 20 people each paid £3·50 for a cinema ticket. How much did they pay altogether? £70

11 $(1^4)^4 =$ 1

12 Does this net make a cube?

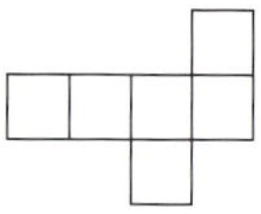

yes

13 What is the perimeter of a rectangle measuring 17 cm × 4 cm? 42 cm

14 Increase £15 by 10%. £16·50

15 Two of the angles in a triangle equal 140°. What is the third angle? 40°

C

1. $\boxed{6} \times 9 = 54$
2. 20 001, 20 000, $\boxed{19\,999}$, 19 998
3. $31 - 16 =$ 15
4. $565 - 328 =$ 237
5. $89 \times 5 =$ 445
6. $37 \div 4 = \boxed{9}$ r 1
7. $74 + 18 =$ 92
8. $1\frac{3}{4} - \frac{1}{4} =$ $1\frac{1}{2}$
9. $3^2 - 4 =$ 5
10. 42 037, 41 937, $\boxed{41\,837}$, 41 737
11. $-17 + 9 - 2 =$ -10
12. $\frac{2}{4} = \frac{\boxed{1}}{2}$
13. $(8 \times 4) + 16 =$ 48
14. $81 \div 6 = \boxed{13}$ r 3
15. 90% of 70 = 63

Draw 3 different shapes with an area of 42 cm^2.

D

1. Write three hundred and eight point five two in numerals. 308·52
2. 3 tenths + 4 units + 7 tens + 8 hundreds = 874·3
3. Round 13·49 to the nearest whole number. 13
4. $27 \times 10 =$ 270
5. Continue the pattern: 36, 23, 10, $\boxed{-3}$, $\boxed{-16}$
6. $3500 \times 30 =$ 105 000
7. Is 105 a multiple of 15? yes
8. What is the volume of a cuboid with sides measuring 4 cm, 5 cm and 6 cm? 120 cm^3
9. A greengrocer had 1762 kg of potatoes. During the day he sold 650 kg of potatoes. How many kg had he left at the end of the day? 1112 kg
10. There are 48 cakes, 4 cakes on each plate. How many plates are there? 12
11. Complete the ratio, 4:48 1:$\boxed{12}$
12. I buy 8 bars of chocolate at 75 p each. How much change do I get from £20? £14
13. What is the area of a shape measuring 8 cm by 20 cm? 160 cm^2
14. Sandwiches in a shop cost 99p, £1·09, £1·29, 99p, £1·06. What is the mode? 99p
15. There are 15 pencils in a box. 5 pencils are yellow. 10 pencils are red. What is the probability of picking a yellow pencil? 5 in 15 or 1 in 3

Exercise 17

A

1 $6 \times \boxed{9} = 54$

2 $\boxed{78\,210}$, 78 211, 78 212, 78 213

3 $55 + 27 + 19 =$ 101

4 $523 + 168 =$ 691

5 $17 \times 9 =$ 153

6 $80 - \boxed{37} = 43$

7 $30 \div 7 = 4 \text{ r } \boxed{2}$

8 $4\frac{1}{3} + \frac{4}{6} =$ 5

9 $3^4 =$ 81

10 $\boxed{70\,988}$, 71 004, 71 020, 71 036

11 $0{\cdot}01 = \boxed{\frac{1}{100}} = \boxed{1}\%$

12 $-18 + 4 =$ −14

13 $(8 \times 9) - 45 =$ 27

14 $59 \div 3 = 19 \text{ r } \boxed{2}$

15 $1{\cdot}4 + 7{\cdot}7 =$ 9·1

What are the co-ordinates for this shape?

(1,0) (2,–1) (3,0) (4,–1) (5,0) (6,–1) (5,–3) (6,–5) (5,–6) (4,–5) (0,–5) (3,–6) (1,–3) (2,–5) (0,–1) (1,–6) (0,–1)

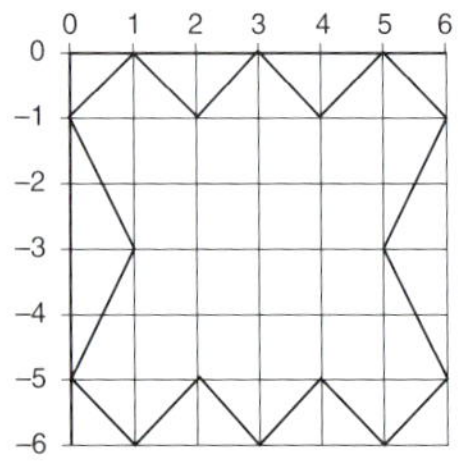

B

1 Write 8093·67 in words.
eight thousand and ninety-three point six seven

2 What value has the 8 in 239·18?
8 hundredths or $\frac{8}{100}$

3 What is the product of 14 and 100? 1400

4 How many times does 14 go into 100? 7 r 2

5 $488 \div 10 =$ 48·8

6 $1500 \div 250 =$ 6

7 Is 9 a factor of 127? No

8 Write 18·45 using the 12 hour clock. 6·45 pm

9 Chris collects postcards. She has 319 from the British Isles and 578 from Europe. How many postcards in her collection? 897

10 It cost 25p for a school raffle ticket. If 20 children buy a ticket, how much money is collected? £5

11 $(2^2)^2 + 3 =$ 19

12 Does this net make a cube?

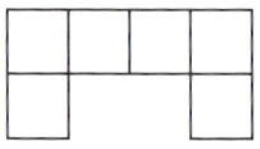

no

13 What is the perimeter of a rectangle measuring 25 m × 4 m? 58 m

14 Increase £20 by 10%. £22

15 Two of the angles in a triangle equal 96°. What is the third angle? 84°

C

1 [9] × 4 = 36

2 [73 200], 73 199, 73 198, 73 197

3 77 – 59 = 18

4 325 – 107 = 218

5 57 × 2 = 114

6 53 ÷ 6 = [8] r 5

7 27 + 64 = 91

8 $2\frac{3}{5} - \frac{4}{5} = 1\frac{4}{5}$

9 $7^2 - 6 = 43$

10 [57 342], 56 342, 55 342, 54 342

11 –13 + 5 – 4 = –12

12 $\frac{12}{16} = \frac{[3]}{4}$

13 (2 × 7) + 14 = 28

14 43 ÷ 3 = [14] r 1

15 20% of 40 = 8

Can you make 89 using +, – and × and all five numbers only once

4	7
59	14
	72

(14 × 7) – 72 + 4 + 59 = 89

D

1 Write five hundred point seven two in numerals. 500·72

2 16 units + 7 tens + 11 thousands + 2 tenths = 11 086·2

3 Round 17·81 to the nearest whole number. 18

4 63·6 × 10 = 636

5 Continue the pattern: 17, 9, 1, [–7], [–15]

6 4500 × 40 = 180 000

7 Is 108 a multiple of 4? yes

8 What is the volume of a cuboid with sides measuring 6 cm, 2 cm and 4 cm? 48 cm^3

9 The warehouse had 5050 dresses. 960 were delivered to a shop. How many were left? 4090

10 70 children are staying to dinner. 5 children sit round each table. How many tables are needed? 14

11 Complete the ratio, 12:72 1:[6]

12 I buy 5 cakes at £1·20 each. How much change do I get from £20? £14

13 What is the area of a plane shape measuring 15 m by 4 m? 60 m^2

14 Ribbons come in these lengths: 50 cm, 125 cm, 100 cm, 125 cm, 100 cm, 125 cm. What is the mode? 125 cm

15 There are 12 coins in a bag. 4 of the coins are silver. What is the probability of picking a silver coin? 4 in 12 or 1 in 3

Exercise 18

A

1. $7 \times \boxed{3} = 21$
2. 69 997, 69 998, 69 999, $\boxed{70\,000}$
3. $63 + 29 + 21 =$ 113
4. $234 + 426 =$ 660
5. $16 \times 6 =$ 96
6. $75 - \boxed{16} = 59$
7. $60 \div 8 = 7$ r $\boxed{4}$
8. $\frac{1}{2} + 3\frac{3}{4} = 4\frac{1}{4}$
9. $4^4 =$ 256
10. 23 509, 23 526, 23 543, $\boxed{23\,560}$
11. $0{\cdot}6 = \boxed{\frac{6}{10}} = \boxed{60}\%$
12. $-11 + 8 =$ -3
13. $(5 \times 10) - 36 =$ 14
14. $71 \div 5 = 14$ r $\boxed{1}$
15. $5{\cdot}5 + 1{\cdot}6 =$ 7·1

B

1. Write 1069·23 in words.
   one thousand and sixty-nine point two three
2. What value has the 8 in 263·86? 8 tenths or $\frac{8}{10}$
3. What is the product of 19 and 20? 380
4. How many times does 18 go into 150? 8 r 6
5. $21663 \div 10 =$ 2166·3
6. $7200 \div 90 =$ 80
7. Is 8 a factor of 116? no
8. Write 23·05 using the 12 hour clock. 11·05 pm
9. The Smith family travel 566 km on Wednesday and 976 km on Thursday. How far do they travel altogether? 1542 km
10. A florist puts 15 daffodils in a bunch. She sells 15 bunches in an hour. How many daffodils is this? 225
11. $(2^3)^2 + 2^2 =$ 68
12. Does this net make a cube? 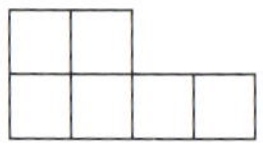
    no
13. What is the perimeter of a rectangle measuring 36 cm × 8 cm? 88 cm
14. Increase £25 by 50%. £37·50
15. Two of the angles in a triangle equal 136°. What is the third angle? 44°

Draw 3 different shapes with a perimeter of 22 cm.

C

1 8 × 6 = 48

2 46 502, 46 501, 46 500, 46 499

3 54 – 38 = 16

4 278 – 159 = 119

5 94 × 3 = 282

6 53 ÷ 7 = 7 r 4

7 57 + 29 = 86

8 $3\frac{2}{5} - \frac{1}{10} = 3\frac{3}{10}$

9 $5^2 - 3 = 22$

10 26 124, 26 024, 25 924, 25 824

11 –11 + 2 – 8 = –17

12 $\frac{8}{14} = \frac{4}{7}$

13 (8 × 6) + 16 = 64

14 33 ÷ 2 = 16 r 1

15 70% of 100 = 70

Copy and complete the Function Machine

× 6

in	out
9	54
12	72
34	204
29	174
16	96
43	258
27	162
31	186
46	276

D

1 Write one thousand and eight point one eight in numerals. 1008·18

2 3 tenths + 4 tens + 12 thousands + 2 units = 12 042·3

3 Round 44·26 to the nearest whole number. 44

4 208 × 10 = 2080

5 Continue the pattern: 17, 5, –7, –19, –31

6 1600 × 50 = 80 000

7 Is 446 a multiple of 4? no

8 What is the volume of a cuboid with sides measuring 4 cm, 5 cm and 3 cm? 60 cm^3

9 A bookshop had 5607 books. 700 are detective novels. How many are not detective novels? 4907

10 The shop has 75 teapots in stock, 15 teapots on each shelf. How many shelves are used? 5

11 Complete the ratio, 16:48 1:3

12 I buy 4 sandwiches at £1·35. How much change do I get from £20? £14·60

13 What is the area of a shape measuring 17 cm by 4 cm? 68 cm^2

14 Children's heights are 1·32 m, 1·34 m, 1·34 m, 1·35 m, 1·31 m, 1·32 m, 1·34 m. What is the mode? 1·34 m

15 There are 12 coins in a bag. 4 of the coins are silver. What is the probability of not picking a silver coin? 8 in 12 or 2 in 3

Exercise 19

A

1. $3 \times$ [9] $= 27$
2. [36 399], 36 400, 36 401, 36 402
3. $42 + 25 + 29 =$ 96
4. $426 + 237 =$ 663
5. $14 \times 8 =$ 112
6. $42 -$ [14] $= 28$
7. $56 \div 6 = 9$ r [2]
8. $1\frac{2}{5} + \frac{4}{5} = 2\frac{1}{5}$
9. $6^3 =$ 216
10. [85 899], 85 911, 85 923, 85 935
11. $0{\cdot}4 = \frac{[4]}{10} =$ [40]%
12. $-13 + 2 =$ -11
13. $(9 \times 9) - 54 =$ 27
14. $110 \div 6 = 18$ r [2]
15. $3{\cdot}4 + 2{\cdot}9 =$ 6·3

Copy and complete.

–	31	22	3	16
29	–2	7	26	13
85	54	63	82	69
43	12	21	40	27
64	33	42	61	48

B

1. Write 4062·73 in words.
   four thousand and sixty-two point seven three
2. What value has the 9 in 364·97? 9 tenths or $\frac{9}{10}$
3. What is the product of 9 and 18? 162
4. How many times does 12 go into 250?
   20 r 10
5. $6713{\cdot}49 \div 10 =$ 671·349
6. $5400 \div 90 =$ 60
7. Is 13 a factor of 78? yes
8. Write 10·25 pm using the 24 hour clock. 22·25
9. On sports day team A scored 685 points and team B scored 688 points.
   How many points did they score altogether?
   1373
10. The school magazine has 9 pages.
    How many pages in 90 copies? 810
11. $(3^2)^2 + 5 =$ 86
12. Does this net make a cube? 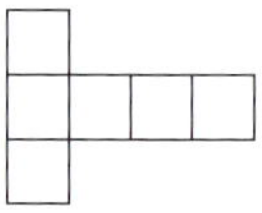
    yes
13. What is the perimeter of a rectangle measuring 45 cm × 8 cm? 106 cm
14. Increase £50 by 10%. £55
15. Two of the angles in a triangle equal 160°.
    What is the third angle? 20°

C

1. [8] × 8 = 64
2. [81 000], 80 999, 80 998, 80 997
3. 93 – 58 = 35
4. 627 – 418 = 209
5. 37 × 6 = 222
6. 47 ÷ 5 = [9] r 2
7. 37 + 48 = 85
8. $1\frac{2}{3} - \frac{1}{6} = 1\frac{1}{2}$ or $1\frac{3}{6}$
9. $8^2 - 8 = 56$
10. 60 830, 60 820, 60 810, [60 800]
11. –18 + 6 – 3 = –15
12. $\frac{3}{6} = \frac{[1]}{2}$
13. (9 × 3) + 19 = 46
14. 75 ÷ 4 = [18] r 3
15. 30% of 110 = 33

Draw 3 different shapes with an area of 36 cm².

D

1. Write six thousand and fourteen point three eight in numerals. 6014·38
2. 2 units + 4 tenths + 16 thousands + 5 tens = 16 052·4
3. Round 58·19 to the nearest whole number. 58
4. 327·6 × 10 = 3276
5. Continue the pattern: 29, 14, –1, [–16], [–31]
6. 3200 × 30 = 96 000
7. Is 756 a multiple of 7? yes
8. What is the volume of a cuboid with sides measuring 8 cm, 2 cm and 3 cm? 48 cm³
9. 2730 bulbs are sown in the park. 870 are daffodils. How many are not daffodils? 1860
10. There are 121 footballers in the competition. There are 11 players in each team. How many teams are taking part? 11
11. Complete the ratio, 13:52 1:[4]
12. I hire 4 video tapes at £2·45 each. How much change do I get from £20? £10·20
13. What is the area of a shape measuring 5 cm by 6 cm? 30 cm²
14. Books have the following number of pages: 235, 337, 237, 335, 237. What is the mode? 237
15. There are 10 pieces of fruit in a bag. 3 pieces are apples. What is the probability of picking an apple? 3 in 10 or 1 in 3

Exercise 20

A

1 $9 \times$ [5] $= 45$

2 91 017, 91 018, 91 019, [91 020]

3 $84 + 16 + 14 =$ 114

4 $347 + 409 =$ 756

5 $19 \times 4 =$ 76

6 $96 -$ [49] $= 47$

7 $25 \div 3 = 8$ r [1]

8 $\frac{1}{2} + 4\frac{1}{4} = 4\frac{3}{4}$

9 $7^3 =$ 343

10 38 459, 38 475, 38 491, [38 507]

11 $0{\cdot}3 = \frac{[3]}{10} =$ [30]%

12 $-19 + 7 =$ −12

13 $(9 \times 4) - 17 =$ 19

14 $149 \div 9 = 16$ r [5]

15 $7{\cdot}3 + 1{\cdot}8 =$ 9·1

What are the co-ordinates for this shape?

(−1,0) (−5,−5) (0,−3) (−4,0) (−2,−6)

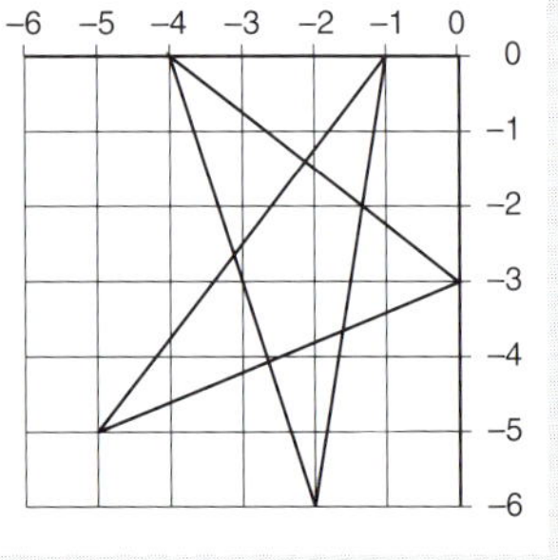

B

1 Write 8095·47 in words.

eight thousand and ninety-five point four seven

2 What value has the 6 in 235·16?

6 hundredths or $\frac{6}{100}$

3 What is the product of 21 and 8? 168

4 How many times does 31 go into 150? 4 r 26

5 $2769{\cdot}72 \div 10 =$ 276·972

6 $8400 \div 70 =$ 120

7 Is 7 a factor of 149? no

8 Write 15·15 using the 12 hour clock. 3·15 pm

9 Tommy walked 746 m to the shop and then 719 m to his friend's house. How far did he walk altogether?

1·465 km

10 If one glass holds 150 ml of lemonade how many ml of lemonade will fill 9 glasses?

1350 ml

11 $(2^3)^3 + 4 =$ 516

12 Does this net make a cube?

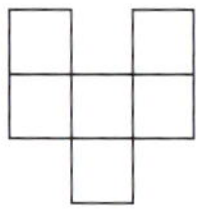

no

13 What is the perimeter of a rectangle measuring 150 cm × 15 cm? 330 cm

14 Increase £50 by 25%. £62·50

15 Two of the angles in a triangle equal 139°. What is the third angle? 41°

C

1. [5] $\times$ 9 = 45
2. 31 200, [31 199], 31 198, 31 197
3. 82 – 67 = 15
4. 793 – 329 = 464
5. 42 $\times$ 4 = 168
6. 45 ÷ 6 = [7] r 3
7. 29 + 43 = 72
8. $2\frac{1}{2} - \frac{1}{4} = 2\frac{1}{4}$
9. $6^2 - 7 = 29$
10. 37 429, 37 419, 37 409, [36 399]
11. –16 + 8 – 4 = –12
12. $\frac{3}{9} = \frac{[1]}{3}$
13. (3 $\times$ 6) + 17 = 35
14. 74 ÷ 5 = [14] r 4
15. 60% of 60 = 36

Can you make 179 using + and $\times$ and all five numbers only once

3	2
17	34
	42

(42 $\times$ 3) + 34 + 17 + 2 = 179

D

1. Write eight hundred and four thousand, seven hundred and ninety-three point four nine in numerals. 804 793·49
2. 4 tens + 6 tenths + 3 units + 2 hundreds + 1 hundredth = 243·61
3. Round 89·68 to the nearest whole number. 90
4. 562·7 $\times$ 10 = 5627
5. Continue the pattern: 49, 24, –1, [–26], [–51]
6. 4900 $\times$ 40 = 196 000
7. Is 637 a multiple of 6? no
8. What is the volume of a cuboid with sides measuring 9 cm, 8 cm and 3 cm? 216 cm^3
9. Rose has £74·53. She spends £8·95 in the art shop. How much money has she left? £65·58
10. There are 105 players in a netball competition. 7 children are in each team. How many teams take part? 15
11. Complete the ratio, 15:75 1:[5]
12. I buy 6 packs of paper cups at 99p each. How much change do I get from £20? £14·06
13. What is the area of a shape measuring 18 m by 4 m? 72 m^2
14. Newspapers cost 30p, 35p, 40p, 40p, 45p and 40p. What is the mode? 40p
15. There are 10 pieces of fruit in a bag. 3 pieces are apples. What is the probability of not picking an apple? 7 in 10 or $\frac{7}{10}$

Exercise 21

A

1. [7] × 3 = 21
2. 134 278, 134 279, [134 280], 134 281
3. 74 + 35 + 28 = 137
4. 235 + 187 = 422
5. 36 × 4 = 144
6. 174 – [28] = 146
7. 34 ÷ 5 = [6] r [4]
8. $1\frac{1}{6} + 2\frac{1}{2} = 3\frac{2}{3}$
9. √81 = 9
10. 465 310, [465 301], 465 292, 465 283
11. 8 – 11 = –3
12. 50% = $\frac{[1]}{[2]}$ = 0·[5]
13. 39 – (3 × 13) = 0
14. 57 ÷ [7] = 8 r 1
15. $\frac{3}{5}$ of 70 = 42

Draw 3 different shapes with a perimeter of 36 cm.

B

1. Write 1033·3 in words.
   one thousand and thirty-three point three
2. 2·3 < 2·29. True or false? false
3. What number is on the bottom of a dice when the 6 is at the top? 1
4. Double 6 plus 4 then find $\frac{1}{2}$ 8
5. 1055 ÷ 100 = 10·55
6. If a compass needle moves from North to South in a clockwise direction, how many degrees does it move through? 180°
7. XIX = 19
8. Approximately how many cm are there in a yard? 90 cm
9. Jane buys 3 games costing £2·99, £3·99 and £10·99.
   How much does she spend? £17·97
10. Mugs are sold in boxes of 15. The café owner buys 4 boxes.
    How many does she get? 60
11. Two thirds of 18 = 12
12. Here is a part of a timetable.

	Depart	Arrive
train A	09·35	10·19
train B	09·55	10·45

    Which train gets there faster, A or B? A
13. What is the perimeter of this shape? 36 cm

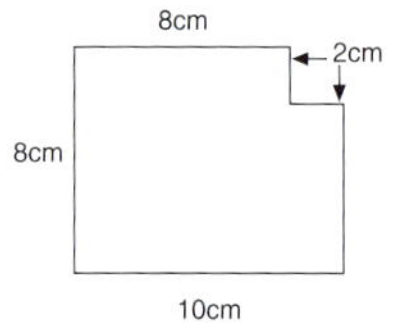

14. Decrease £50 by 50%.
    £25
15. Two of the angles in a triangle are 45° and 55°.
    What is the third angle? 80°

C

1 $4 \times$ [4] $= 16$

2 127 543, 127 542, 127 541, [127 540]

3 $24{\cdot}6 \times 10 =$ 246

4 $428 - 139 =$ 289

5 $32 \times 10 =$ 320

6 $86 \div 7 =$ [12] r [2]

7 $29 +$ [39] $= 68$

8 $3\frac{5}{8} - 2\frac{1}{4} =$ $1\frac{3}{8}$

9 $2^3 + 4 =$ 12

10 424 581, 425 581, 426 581, [427 581]

11 $12 - 28 =$ –16

12 $\frac{12}{7} =$ $1\frac{5}{7}$

13 $53 + (14 \times 2) =$ 81

14 $65 \div 4 =$ 16 r 1

15 $7{\cdot}35 + 2{\cdot}47 =$ 9·82

Copy and complete the Function Machine

+ 32

in	out
35	67
27	59
16	48
41	73
29	61
32	64
10	42
46	78
59	91

D

1 Write seventeen thousand eight hundred and fifty-seven point nine in numerals.
17 857·9

2 $23 + 48 < 37 + 51$. True or false? true

3 Round 17·396 to two decimal places. 17·40

4 $0{\cdot}56 \times 100 =$ 56

5 Which is larger, 2^3 of 3^2? 3^2

6 Write 16 in roman numerals. XVI

7 Put these numbers in order, largest first: 2·14, 4·21, 12·4 12·4, 4·21, 2·14

8 What is the square root of 49? 7

9 The school library owns 2788 books. This week 1879 books are in the library. How many have been borrowed? 909

10 How many programmes lasting 24 minutes can fit onto a 240-minute video tape? 10

11 What is 50% expressed as a ratio? 1:2

12 How much change from £20 do I get if I buy 2 books at £3·50 each and a magazine for £1·95? £11·05

13 What is the area of this shape? 28 cm²

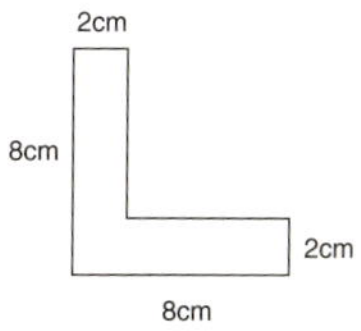

14 What is the mean average of these numbers: 16, 14, 18? 16

15 If I roll a dice marked from 7–12, what chance do I have of throwing an even number? 1 in 2 or evens

Exercise 22

A

1. 8 × 4 = 32
2. 256 498, 256 499, 256 500, 256 501
3. 35 + 46 + 25 = 106
4. 167 + 355 = 522
5. 27 × 9 = 243
6. 328 – 109 = 219
7. 40 ÷ 6 = 6 r 4
8. $2\frac{1}{2} + 3\frac{1}{4} = 5\frac{3}{4}$
9. √16 = 4
10. 258 392, 258 378, 258 364, 259 350
11. 7 – 13 = –6
12. $75\% = \frac{3}{4} = 0{\cdot}75$
13. 127 – (4 × 12) = 79
14. 66 ÷ 8 = 8 r 2
15. $\frac{5}{6}$ of 42 = 35

Copy and complete.

×	84	72	60	36
$\frac{1}{4}$	21	18	15	9
$\frac{1}{2}$	42	36	30	18
$\frac{3}{4}$	63	54	45	27
$\frac{2}{3}$	56	48	40	24

B

1. Write 15 001·9 in words.
   fifteen thousand and one point nine
2. 2·45 > 2·5. True or false? false
3. What is the number on the bottom of a dice when the 3 is at the top? 4
4. Treble 7 minus 3, then find $\frac{1}{3}$ 6
5. 1878 ÷ 100 = 18·78
6. A compass needle moves anti-clockwise from South to East. How many degrees does it move through? 90°
7. XXIV = 24
8. Approximately how many kg are there in a lb (pound)? 0·4
9. I went on a 3-day journey. I went 421 km, 452 km and 478 km. How far did I travel? 1351 km
10. Potatoes are planted in rows of 14. The gardener sows 3 rows. How many plants? 42
11. Three quarters of 40 = 30
12. Here is a part of a timetable.

	Depart	Arrive
train A	11·57	12.45
train B	12·17	13.05

If train B travels at the same rate as train A, when will it arrive?

13. What is the perimeter of this shape? 72 cm

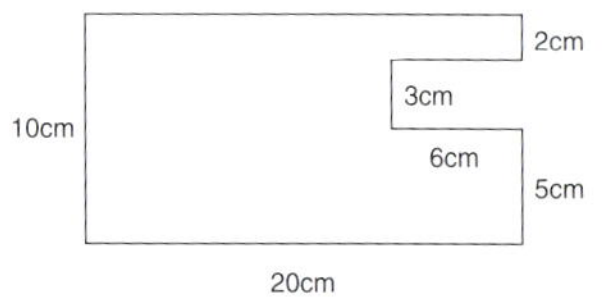

14. Decrease £25 by 50%. £12·50
15. Two of the angles in a triangle are 87° and 48°. What is the third angle? 45°

C

1 $2 \times$ [10] $= 20$

2 346 540, [346 539], 346 538, 346 537

3 $3{\cdot}78 \times 10 =$ 37·8

4 $342 - 175 =$ 167

5 $44 \times 10 =$ 440

6 $115 \div 8 =$ [14] r [3]

7 $38 +$ [35] $= 73$

8 $4\frac{2}{5} - 3\frac{3}{4} = \frac{13}{20}$

9 $3^3 + 7 =$ 34

10 378 492, 379 492, [380 492], 381 492

11 $14 - 27 =$ –13

12 $\frac{15}{8} = 1\frac{7}{8}$

13 $42 + (13 \times 2) =$ 68

14 $42 \div 3 =$ 14

15 $5{\cdot}42 + 3{\cdot}29 =$ 8·71

Draw 3 different shapes with an area of $12\,cm^2$.

D

1 Write twenty-nine thousand and eight point four in numerals. 29 008·4

2 27 + 54 > 38 + 43. True or false? false

3 Round 18·792 to two decimal places. 18·79

4 $0{\cdot}87 \times 100 =$ 87

5 Which is smaller, 4^2 or 33? 4^2

6 Write 28 in roman numerals. XXVIII

7 Put these numbers in order, smallest first: 42, 51·7, 23·9. 23·9, 42, 51·7

8 What is the square root of 81? 9

9 A factory produces 4876 chocolate bars an hour. 1472 of these are milk chocolate, how many are plain? 3404

10 How many 10-minute appointments can a doctor's receptionist make in 2 hours 25 minutes? 14

11 What is 25% expressed as a ratio? 1:4

12 What change do I get from £20 if I buy 3 sandwiches at 75p each and a can of orange for 50p? £17·25

13 What is the area of this shape? $23\,cm^2$

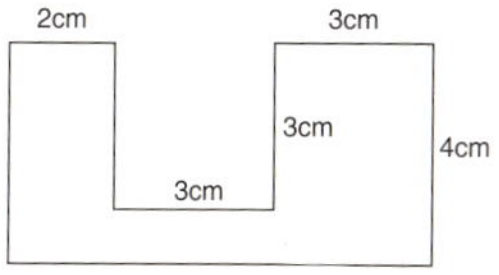

14 What is the mean average of these numbers: 11, 9, 16? 12

15 There are 24 cubes in a bag. There are 18 green and 6 blue. What is the probability of not pulling out a green cube? 6 in 24 or 1 in 4

Exercise 23

A

1. [8] × 7 = 56
2. 497 375, 497 376, 497 377, [497 378]
3. 56 + 37 + 22 = 115
4. 529 + 278 = 807
5. 66 × 8 = 528
6. 437 – [109] = 328
7. 29 ÷ 4 = [7] r [1]
8. $4\frac{1}{4} + 2\frac{3}{8} = 6\frac{5}{8}$
9. √36 = 6
10. 558 587, 558 571, 558 555, [558 539]
11. 6 – 9 = –3
12. 20% = $\frac{[1]}{[5]}$ = 0·[2]
13. 132 – (15 × 7) = 27
14. 66 ÷ [7] = 9 r 3
15. $\frac{3}{7}$ of 63 = 27

What are the co-ordinates for this shape?

(0,–3) (–1,5) (–2,–4) (–3,–6) (–4,–4) (–5,–5) (–6,–3) (–5,–1) (–2,–2) (–4,–2) (–1,–1) (–3,0)

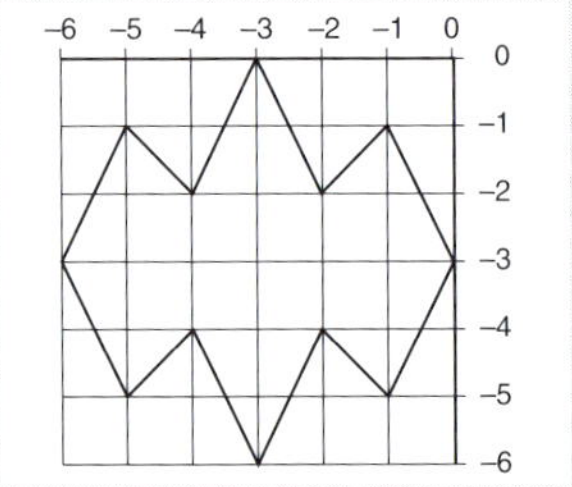

B

1. Write 26 400·2 in words.
   twenty-six thousand and four hundred point two
2. 2·32 < 2·2. True or false? false
3. I throw a dice. It has a 2 on the top.
   What is the number on the opposite face? 5
4. Treble 8, plus 6 then find $\frac{1}{5}$ 6
5. 30·75 ÷ 100 = 0·3075
6. If a compass needle moves clockwise from North to South-East, how many degrees does it move through? 135°
7. XXXIV = 34
8. Approximately how many pints are there in a litre? 1·75 or $1\frac{3}{4}$
9. School A has 561 children. School B has 229 children. School C has 175 children. How many children altogether? 965
10. There are 4 rows of children in the hall, 13 in each row. How many in total? 52
11. Four fifths of 25 = 20
12. Here is a part of a timetable.

	Depart	Arrive
train A	13·27	14·02
train B	15·22	15·57

   What time does train A leave if both journeys take the same time?
13. What is the perimeter of this shape? 106 cm

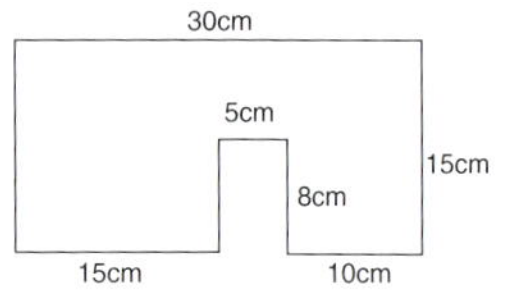

14. Decrease £20 by 25%.
   £15
15. Two of the angles in a triangle are 68° and 35°.
   What is the third angle? 77°

C

1. $3 \times \boxed{7} = 21$
2. 609 011, 609 010, [609 009], 609 008
3. $251 \times 100 = 25100$
4. $217 - 128 = 89$
5. $28 \times 100 = 2800$
6. $100 \div 6 = \boxed{16}$ r $\boxed{4}$
7. $57 + \boxed{37} = 94$
8. $7\frac{2}{7} - 4\frac{3}{5} = 2\frac{24}{35}$
9. $4^3 + 8 = 72$
10. 622 407, 621 407, 620 407, [619 407]
11. $17 - 32 = -15$
12. $\frac{16}{5} = 3\frac{1}{5}$
13. $29 + (15 \times 3) = 74$
14. $97 \div 6 = 16$ r 1
15. $2{\cdot}37 + 1{\cdot}34 = 3{\cdot}71$

Can you make 1672 using – and × and all five numbers only once

5	4
	21
46	
	37

$(46 \times 37) - 21 - 9 = 1672$

D

1. Write twenty-six thousand four hundred and one point three in numerals. 26 401·3
2. $63 + 17 < 58 + 29$. True or false? true
3. Round 18·149 to two decimal places. 18·15
4. $9{\cdot}26 \times 100 = 926$
5. Which is larger, 2^3 or 4^2? 4^2
6. Write 38 in Roman numerals. XXXVIII
7. Put these numbers in order, largest first: 8·13, 8·3, 8·31 8·31, 8·3, 8·13
8. What is the cube root of 8? 2
9. A tea urn holds 2175 ml. Mrs White pours out 1782 ml. How much is left? 393 ml
10. How many booklets of 4 pages can be made from 94 sheets of paper? 23
11. What is 20% expressed as a ratio? 1:5
12. How much change do I get from £20 if I buy 2 sandwiches at £1·20 each and 2 cakes at 60p each? £16·40
13. What is the area of this shape? 18 m^2

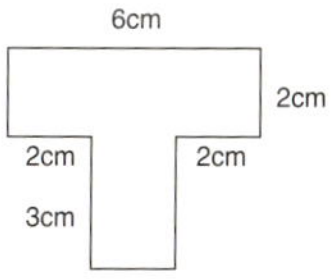

14. What is the mean average of these numbers: 12, 18, 18? 16
15. If I roll a dice marked from 7–12, what chance do I have of throwing a number higher than 8? 1 in 2 or 3 in 6

Exercise 24

A

1 [7] × 6 = 42

2 [802 261], 802 262, 802 263, 802 264

3 42 + 37 + 29 = 108

4 354 + 459 = 813

5 58 × 4 = 232

6 235 – [109] = 126

7 28 ÷ 3 = [9] r [1]

8 $4\frac{1}{6} + 2\frac{2}{3} = 6\frac{5}{6}$

9 √25 = 5

10 [284 020], 284 008, 283 996, 283 984

11 14 – 20 = –6

12 10% = $\frac{[1]}{[10]}$ = 0·[1]

13 143 – (8 × 16) = 15

14 39 ÷ [6] = 6 r 3

15 $\frac{5}{8}$ of 64 = 40

Draw 3 different shapes with a perimeter of 40 cm.

B

1 Write 35 480·7 in words.
Thirty-five thousand, four hundred and eighty point seven

2 13·89 > 18·90. True or false? false

3 If there is a 1 on the top of a dice, what number is on the opposite face? 5

4 Double 20 minus 8, then find $\frac{1}{4}$ 8

5 10786 ÷ 100 = 107·86

6 If a compass needle moves anti-clockwise from West to North-East, how many degrees does in move through? 135°

7 XC = 90

8 Approximately how many cm are there in an inch? 2·5 cm

9 Lorna buys 3 items at £8·50, £2·95 and £3·55.
How much does she spend? £15·00

10 How many eggs in 12 dozen? 144

11 Seven eighths of 56 = 49

12 Here is a part of a timetable.

	Depart	Arrive
train A	17·55	18·45
train B	18·25	19·15

When does train A leave if both journeys take the same time?

13 What is the perimeter of this shape? 90 cm

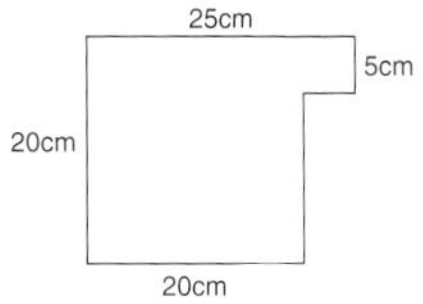

14 Decrease £20 by 10%.
£18

15 Two of the angles in a triangle are 55° and 38°. What is the third angle? 87°

C

1. $7 \times \boxed{6} = 42$
2. 269 000, $\boxed{268\,999}$, 268 998, 268 997
3. $3{\cdot}52 \times 100 = 352$
4. $576 - 288 = 288$
5. $48 \times 100 = 4800$
6. $69 \div 4 = \boxed{17}$ r $\boxed{1}$
7. $46 + \boxed{36} = 82$
8. $2\frac{3}{4} - 1\frac{1}{2} = 1\frac{1}{4}$
9. $2^3 - 5 = 3$
10. 219 584, 209 584, $\boxed{199\,584}$, 189 584
11. $15 - 34 = -19$
12. $\frac{13}{7} = 1\frac{6}{7}$
13. $37 + (14 \times 3) = 79$
14. $73 \div 5 = 14$ r 3
15. $5{\cdot}19 + 2{\cdot}45 = 7{\cdot}64$

Copy and complete the Function Machine

$\times 3 + 1$

in	out
6	19
12	37
15	46
17	52
21	64
37	112
46	139
29	88
35	106

D

1. Write thirty-five thousand two hundred point six in numerals. 35 200·6
2. 54 – 17 < 45 – 9. True or false? false
3. Round 46·9435 to two decimal places. 49·94
4. $33{\cdot}69 \times 100 = 3369$
5. Which is smaller, 3^3 or 4^2? 4^2
6. Write 48 in roman numerals. XLVIII
7. Put these numbers in order, largest first: 3·14, 3·72, 3·8 3·8, 3·72, 3·14
8. What is the square root of 25? 5
9. Anne has £28·62 to spend. After her shopping trip she has £11·95 left. How much has she spent? £16·67
10. If 108 children join a rounders tournament. They are put into teams of 9. How many teams are there? 12
11. What is 33% expressed as a ratio? 1:3
12. How much change do I get from £20 if I buy 2 notebooks at £1·25 each and 2 pens at £1·75 each? £14
13. What is the area of this shape? 13 cm^2

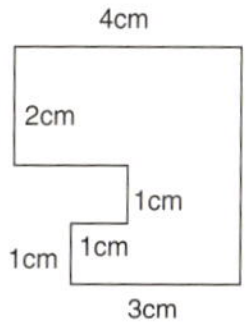

14. What is the mean average of these numbers: 24, 14, 13? 17
15. There are 6 bulbs planted in a bowl. They are a mixture of daffodils and tulips. How many different combinations could there be? 5

Exercise 25

A

1 $\boxed{3} \times 9 = 27$

2 248 478, 248 479, $\boxed{248\,480}$, 248 481

3 $19 + 38 + 73 =$ 130

4 $655 + 365 =$ 1020

5 $72 \times 5 =$ 360

6 $153 - \boxed{18} = 135$

7 $56 \div 6 = \boxed{9}$ r $\boxed{2}$

8 $3\frac{2}{3} + 4\frac{2}{3} = 8\frac{1}{3}$

9 $\sqrt{49} =$ 7

10 728 206, $\boxed{728\,191}$, 728 176, 728 161

11 $9 - 17 =$ −8

12 $25\% = \frac{\boxed{1}}{\boxed{4}} = 0{\cdot}\boxed{25}$

13 $128 - (14 \times 6) =$ 44

14 $37 \div \boxed{5} = 7$ r 2

15 $\frac{3}{4}$ of 40 = 30

Copy and complete.

%	30	40	50	90
30	9	12	15	27
50	15	20	25	45
60	18	24	30	54
75	22·5	30	37·5	67·5

B

1 Write 87 008·6 in words.
eighty-seven thousand and eight point six

2 $23{\cdot}08 < 23{\cdot}50$. True or false? true

3 I throw 2 dice. The numbers on the top are 5 and 3. What are the numbers on the opposite faces? 2 and 4

4 Treble 12, plus 4 then find $\frac{1}{4}$ 10

5 $20932 \div 100 =$ 209·32

6 If a compass needle moves clockwise from South-East to North-East, how many degrees does it move through? 270°

7 XL = 40

8 Approximately how many grams are there in an ounce? 0·04

9 Tom mixes 525 g of flour, 270 g of sugar and 450 g of margarine. What is the total weight of the mixture? 1245 g

10 The librarian puts 12 new books in each pile. There are 11 piles of new books. How many new books altogether? 132

11 Five sixths of 30 = 25

12 Here is a part of a timetable.

	Depart	Arrive
train A	09·28	10·17
train B	11·53	12·35

Which train is quicker, A or B? B

13 What is the perimeter of this shape? 32 cm

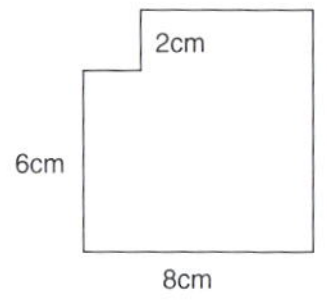

14 Decrease £30 by 20%. £24

15 Two of the angles in a triangle are 63° and 68°. What is the third angle? 49°

C

1 $8 \times$ 8 $= 64$

2 730 531, 730 530, 730 529, 730 528

3 $302 \times 10 =$ 3020

4 $715 - 438 =$ 277

5 $100 \times 33 =$ 3300

6 $147 \div 9 =$ 16 r 3

7 $27 +$ 46 $= 73$

8 $4\frac{3}{15} - 1\frac{1}{5} =$ 3

9 $4^3 - 7 =$ 57

10 540 326, 539 326, 538 326, 537 326

11 $18 - 29 =$ −11

12 $\frac{17}{9} =$ $1\frac{8}{9}$

13 $51 + (13 \times 3) =$ 90

14 $134 \div 9 =$ 14 r 8

15 $6{\cdot}27 + 1{\cdot}78 =$ 8·05

Draw 3 different shapes with an area of 18 cm^2.

D

1 Write forty-seven thousand and forty-nine point one in numerals. 47 049·1

2 $78 - 39 > 68 - 27$ True or false? false

3 Round 118·612 to two decimal places. 118·61

4 $101{\cdot}57 \times 100 =$ 10 157

5 Which is smaller, 2^5 or 3^3? 3^3

6 Write 88 in roman numerals. LXXXVIII

7 Put these numbers in order, largest first: 2·14, 2·3, 2·12. 2·3, 2·14, 2·12

8 What is the square root of 64? 8

9 A shop has 7295 tins of paint. After a week they have 5886 tins left. How many tins have been sold? 1409

10 How many packs of 12 pencils can be made from 150 pencils? 12

11 What is 10% expressed as a ratio? 1:10

12 How much change do I get from £20 if I buy 2 bottles of bubble bath at £1·95 and a soap at 85p? £15·25

13 What is the area of the unshaded section? 42 m^2

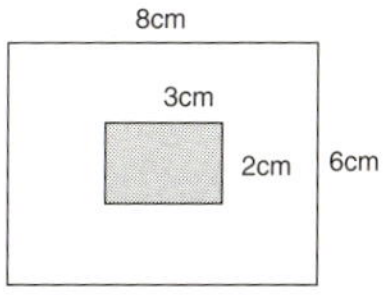

14 What is the mean average of these numbers: 12, 37, 23? 24

15 There are 18 chocolates in a box. 12 of these are hard centres and 6 are soft centres. What is the probability of not picking a soft centre? 12 in 18 or $\frac{2}{3}$

Exercise 26

A

1 [8] × 3 = 24

2 [364 064], 364 065, 364 066, 364 067

3 84 + 57 + 27 = 168

4 743 + 288 = 1031

5 82 × 2 = 164

6 237 – [118] = 119

7 67 ÷ 8 = [8] r [3]

8 $1\frac{1}{5} + 3\frac{2}{10} = 4\frac{2}{5}$

9 √4 = 2

10 [835 514], 835 497, 835 480, 835 463

11 10 – 19 = –9

12 1% = $\frac{[1]}{[100]}$ = 0·[01]

13 117 – (2 × 16) = 85

14 86 ÷ [9] = 9 r 5

15 $\frac{1}{3}$ of 27 = 9

What are the co-ordinates for this shape?

(–5,5) (–4,5) (–3,4) (–2,5) (–1,5) (–2,4) (–1,3) (–2,2) (–1,1) (–2,1) (–3,2) (–4,1) (–5,1) (–4,2) (–5,3) (–4,4)

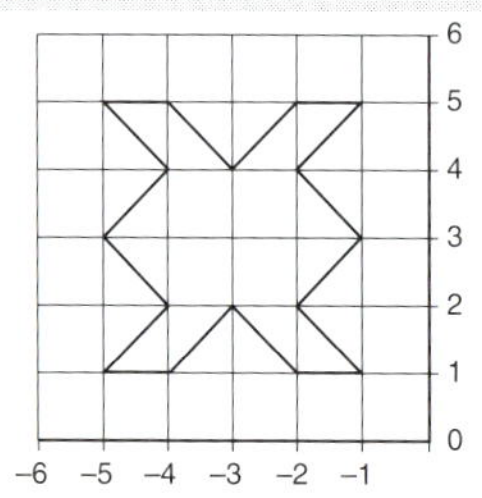

B

1 Write 10 728·69 in words.
ten thousand seven hundred and twenty-eight point six nine

2 18·67 > 18·76. True or false? false

3 I throw 2 dice. The numbers on the top are 5 and 4. What is the total of the numbers on the opposite faces? 5

4 Half 48 plus 6, then find $\frac{1}{3}$ 10

5 2078 ÷ 100 = 20·78

6 If a compass needle moves anti-clockwise from South-East to South-West, how many degrees does it move through? 270°

7 LXXI = 71

8 Approximately how many km are there in a mile? 1·6 or $1\frac{3}{5}$

9 In the library, there are 320 picture books, 490 stories, and 495 non-fiction. How many books altogether? 1305

10 There are 12 shelves of videos, 7 to a shelf. How many videos are there? 84

11 Five ninths of 72 = 40

12 Here is a part of a timetable.

	Depart	Arrive
train A	16·43	18·06
train B	18·49	20·14

Which train is faster, A or B? A

13 What is the perimeter of this shape? 94 cm

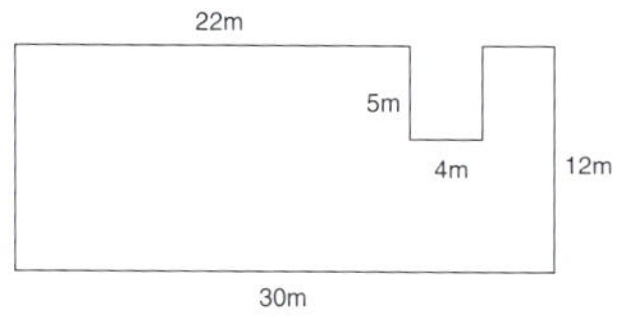

14 Decrease £25 by 20%.
£20

15 Two of the angles in a triangle are 48° and 62°. What is the third angle? 70°

C

1 $9 \times$ [7] $= 63$

2 911 111, [911 110], 911 109, 911 108

3 $10 \times 5{\cdot}43 =$ 54·3

4 $421 - 242 =$ 179

5 $10 \times 63 =$ 630

6 $56 \div 3 =$ [18] r [2]

7 $39 +$ [52] $= 91$

8 $3\frac{3}{5} - 1\frac{1}{3} = 2\frac{4}{15}$

9 $2^3 + 8 =$ 16

10 [717 906], 707 906, 697 906, 687 906

11 $20 - 35 =$ −15

12 $\frac{19}{3} = 6\frac{1}{3}$

13 $27 + (15 \times 2) =$ 57

14 $102 \div 6 =$ 17

15 $3{\cdot}46 + 1{\cdot}39 =$ 4·85

Can you make 214 using +, – and × and all five numbers only once

8 3 26 27 31

$(27 \times 8) + 26 - 31 + 3 = 214$

D

1 Write one hundred and one thousand six hundred and four point two seven in numerals. 101 604·27

2 $108 + 67 > 125 + 48$. True or false? true

3 Round 7·63791 to two decimal places. 7·64

4 $37{\cdot}49 \times 10 =$ 374·9

5 Which is larger, 7^2 or 2^5? 2^5

6 Write 89 in roman numerals. LXXXIX

7 Put these numbers in order, smallest first: 16·52, 12·7, 13·28 12·7, 13·28, 16·52

8 What is the square root of 16? 4

9 The first leg of a journey is 2796 km. If the total length of the journey is 5887, how long is the second leg? 3091

10 Glue sticks need to be packed in boxes of 12. How many boxes can be filled from 200 glue sticks? 16

11 What is 30% expressed as a ratio? 1:3

12 How much change do I get from £20 if I buy 2 candlesticks at £3·75 each and 2 candles at 75p each? £11

13 What is the area of the unshaded section? 182 m²

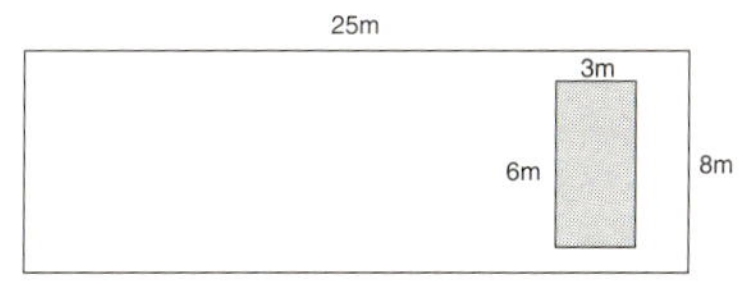

14 What is the mean average of these numbers: 25, 16, 25? 22

15 If I roll a dice marked from 13–18, what chance have I got of scoring less than 16? 1 in 2 or evens

Exercise 27

A

1 9 $\times$ 5 = 45

2 741 597, 741 598, 741 599, 741 600

3 53 + 22 + 48 = 123

4 823 + 198 = 1021

5 94 $\times$ 6 = 564

6 528 – 219 = 309

7 44 $\div$ 7 = 6 r 2

8 $5\frac{4}{5} + 2\frac{2}{5} = 8\frac{1}{5}$

9 $\sqrt{144}$ = 12

10 178 592, 178 579, 178 566, 178 553

11 17 – 21 = –4

12 33% = $\frac{1}{3}$ = 0·33

13 78 – (13 $\times$ 4) = 26

14 28 $\div$ 3 = 9 r 1

15 $\frac{5}{9}$ of 72 = 40

Draw 3 different shapes with a perimeter of 24 cm.

B

1 Write 20 963·62 in words.
twenty thousand and nine hundred sixty-three point six two

2 108·29 < 108·92. True or false? true

3 I throw 2 dice. I score 3 and 6. What is the total of the numbers on the opposite faces? 5

4 Double 22 plus 6, then find $\frac{1}{5}$ 10

5 327·8 $\div$ 100 = 3·278

6 If a compass needle moves clockwise from South to North-West, how many degrees does it move through? 135°

7 C in roman numerals = 100

8 Approximately how many feet in a metre? $3\frac{1}{4}$

9 Sarah cuts a long ribbon into three lengths: 228 cm, 498 cm and 627 cm.
How long was the original piece of ribbon?
1353 cm or 13 m 53 cm

10 There are 14 marbles in each bag.
Edward has 5 bags.
How many marbles does he have? 70

11 Seven eighths of 64 = 56

12 Here is a part of a timetable.

	Depart	Arrive
train A	20·32	21·19
train B	21·08	21·55

If both journeys take the same time, when does train B arrive?

13 What is the perimeter of this shape? 84 cm

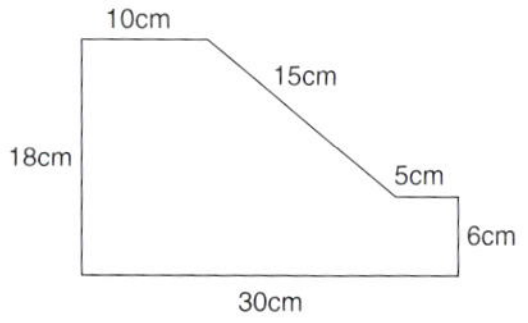

14 Decrease £80 by 25%.
£60

15 Two of the angles in a triangle are 57° and 65°. What is the third angle? 58°

C

1 $5 \times \boxed{5} = 25$

2 408 572, 408 571, 408 570, $\boxed{408\,569}$

3 $4{\cdot}29 \times 10 =$ 42·9

4 $605 - 228 =$ 377

5 $69 \times 1000 =$ 69 000

6 $132 \div 7 = \boxed{18}$ r $\boxed{6}$

7 $58 + \boxed{24} = 82$

8 $4\frac{1}{4} - 2\frac{1}{2} = 1\frac{3}{4}$

9 $3^3 - 8 =$ 19

10 935 242, 835 242, $\boxed{735\,242}$, 635 242

11 $13 - 24 =$ −11

12 $\frac{14}{8} = 1\frac{6}{8}$ or $1\frac{3}{4}$

13 $33 + (14 \times 2) =$ 61

14 $107 \div 8 =$ 13 r 3

15 $3{\cdot}15 + 2{\cdot}48 =$ 5·63

Copy and complete the Function Machine
+ 5 × 2

in	out
16	42
21	52
9	28
14	38
27	64
31	72
48	106
34	78
52	114

D

1 Write two hundred thousand seven hundred and fifty point seven five in numerals. 200 750·75

2 $5 \times 19 < 4 \times 21$. True or false? false

3 Round 10·45297 to two decimal places. 10·45

4 $107{\cdot}62 \times 10 =$ 1076·2

5 Which is smaller, 8^2 or 3^3? 3^3

6 Write 101 in roman numerals. CI

7 Put these numbers in order, smallest first: 70·23, 7·2, 7·23   7·2, 7·23, 70·23

8 What is the cube root of 64? 4

9 9753 books have been sorted into fiction and non-fiction. If there are 549 fiction books, how many non-fiction are there? 9204

10 Candles are sold in boxes of 8. How many boxes can be filled from 100 candles? 12

11 What is $12\frac{1}{2}\%$ expressed as a ratio? 1:8

12 How much change do I get from £20 if I buy a CD at £12·99 and a book at £3·50? £3·51

13 What is the area of this shape? 43 cm^2

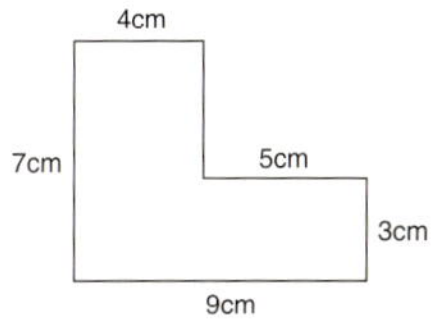

14 What is the mean average of these numbers: 8, 9, 18, 5? 10

15 I have a mixture of 4 red and blue socks in a bag. How many different combinations might there be? 3

Exercise 28

A

1. [5] × 8 = 40
2. 710 638, 710 639, [710 640], 710 641
3. 28 + 59 + 34 = 121
4. 638 + 373 = 1011
5. 46 × 3 = 138
6. 625 − [208] = 417
7. 38 ÷ 4 = [9] r [2]
8. $3\frac{4}{6} + 1\frac{1}{3} = 5$
9. √100 = 10
10. 349 136, 349 118, [349 100], 349 082
11. 16 − 24 = −8
12. 70% = $\frac{[7]}{[10]}$ = 0·[7]
13. 90 − (5 × 16) = 10
14. 80 ÷ [11] = 7 r 3
15. $\frac{2}{5}$ of 45 = 18

Copy and complete.

+	32	47	29	48
45	77	92	74	93
87	119	134	116	135
56	88	103	85	104
73	105	120	102	121

B

1. Write 10 808·09 in words.
   ten thousand and eight hundred and eight point zero nine
2. 21·21 > 21·30. True or false? false
3. I throw 2 dice and score a 5 and a 1.
   What is the total of the opposite faces? 8
4. Half 86 plus 7, then find $\frac{1}{3}$ 16·66
5. 2802 ÷ 100 = 28·02
6. If a compass needle moves anti-clockwise from North to North-West, how many degrees does it move through? 45°
7. M in roman numerals = 1000
8. Approximately how many cm are there in a foot? 30
9. Three children playing Canasta scored 585, 602 and 493 points. How many points did they score altogether? 1680
10. Jason fits 14 buns on each baking tray. He fills 4 trays.
    How many buns does he make? 56
11. Three quarters of 120? 90
12. Here is a part of a timetable.

	Depart	Arrive
train A	13·19	15·07
train B	14·25	16·03

How long does each journey take?
1 hr 48 min and 1 hr 38 min

13. What is the perimeter of this shape? 102 cm

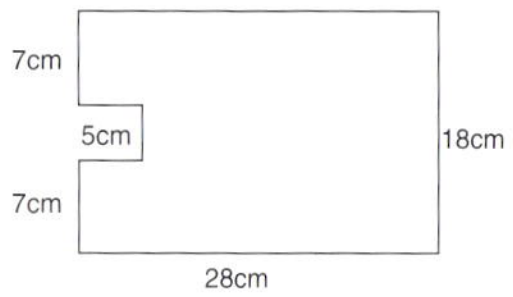

14. Decrease £90 by 10%. £81
15. Two of the angles in a triangle are 36° and 36°.
    What is the third angle? 108°

C

1 $8 \times \boxed{4} = 32$

2 814 240, $\boxed{814\,239}$, 814 238, 814 237

3 $4{\cdot}07 \times 10 =$ 40·7

4 $932 - 547 =$ 385

5 $94 \times 10 =$ 940

6 $129 \div 8 = \boxed{16}$ r $\boxed{1}$

7 $49 + \boxed{24} = 73$

8 $3\frac{3}{10} - 1\frac{2}{5} = 1\frac{9}{10}$

9 $2^3 - 4 =$ 4

10 $\boxed{459\,076}$, 458 976, 458 876, 458 776

11 $16 - 32 =$ –16

12 $\frac{15}{9} = 1\frac{6}{9}$ or $1\frac{2}{3}$

13 $48 + (12 \times 3) =$ 84

14 $51 \div 3 =$ 17

15 $4{\cdot}76 + 2{\cdot}59 =$ 7·35

Draw 3 different shapes with an area of 40 cm^2.

D

1 Write five hundred thousand and one point nine seven in numerals. 500 001·97

2 $108 \div 4 > 110 \div 5$. True or false? true

3 Round 63·279412 to two decimal places. 63·28

4 $101{\cdot}23 \times 10 =$ 1012·3

5 Which is larger, 10^2 or 3^4? 10^2

6 Write 750 in roman numerals. DCCL

7 Put these numbers in order, largest first: 103·47, 103·7, 103·4 103·7, 103·47, 103·4

8 What is the cube root of 16? 2

9 A greengrocer had 9729 apples delivered. 4895 of them are red, the rest are green. How many are green? 4834

10 How many 35 minute programmes will fit onto a 4 hour video tape? 6

11 What is 5% expressed as a ratio? 1:20

12 How much change from £20 do I get if I buy 2 tubs of luxury ice-cream at £3·49 each and a pizza at £6·25? £6·77

13 What is the area of this shape? 40 cm^2

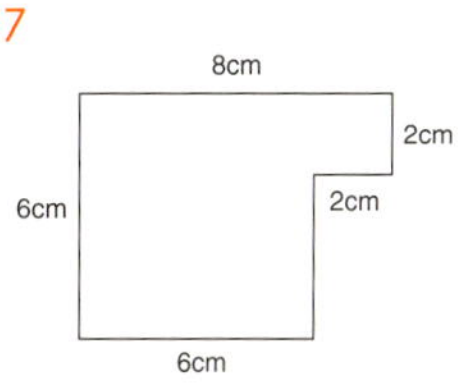

14 What is the mean average of these numbers: 22, 7, 16, 15? 15

15 There are 15 jellies in a bag. 3 are orange flavour, 2 are lime, and the rest are raspberry. What is the probability of picking a raspberry one? 10 in 15 or $\frac{2}{3}$

Exercise 29

A

1. [3] × 6 = 18
2. 582 309, 582 310, [582 311], 582 312
3. 67 + 43 + 17 = 127
4. 757 + 264 = 1021
5. 65 × 7 = 455
6. 364 – [118] = 246
7. 85 ÷ 9 = [9] r [4]
8. $4\frac{1}{2} + 2\frac{3}{4} = 7\frac{1}{4}$
9. √64 = 8
10. 369 217, 369 201, [369 185], 369 169
11. 15 – 26 = –11
12. $3\% = \frac{[3]}{[100]} = 0{\cdot}[03]$
13. 100 – (17 × 3) = 49
14. 47 ÷ [9] = 5 r 2
15. $\frac{2}{3}$ of 24 = 16

What are the co-ordinates for this shape?

(4,0) (6,–2) (5,–3) (6,–4) (4,–6) (2,–4) (4,–2) (2,0) (0,–2) (1,–3) (0,–4) (2,–6) (4,–4) (2,–2)

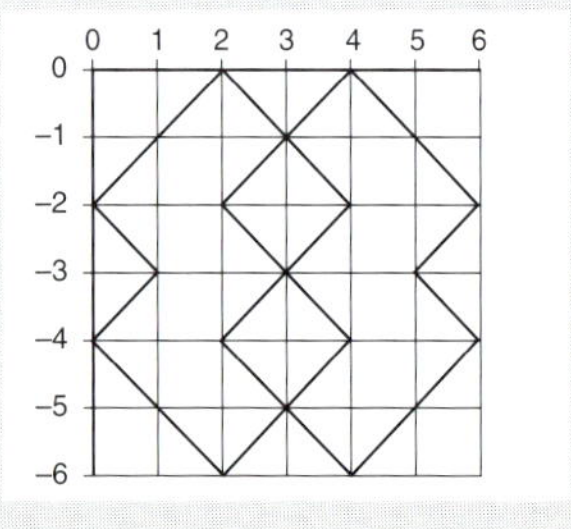

B

1. Write 1273·8 in words.
   one thousand two hundred and seventy-three point eight
2. 208·08 > 280·80. True or false? false
3. I throw 3 dice. I score 2, 4, 3.
   What is the total of the opposite faces? 12
4. Double 18 minus 4, then find $\frac{1}{8}$ 4
5. 20703 ÷ 100 = 207·03
6. If a compass needle moves anti-clockwise from East to South-West, how many degrees does it move through? 225°
7. MCM in roman numerals = 1900
8. Approximately how many kg are there in a stone? 6·3
9. Three farmers have 739, 867, and 496 sheep each. How many sheep is this? 2102
10. There are 15 photographs in each of Hannah's 6 albums.
    How many photographs has she? 90
11. Nine tenths of 180. 162
12. Here is a part of a timetable.

	Depart	Arrive
train A	18·49	20·33
train B	19·19	21·03

    If both journeys are the same length, when did train B leave?
13. What is the perimeter of this shape? 102 cm

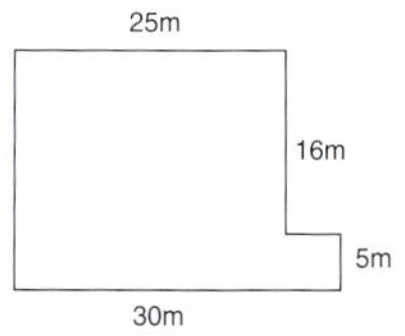

14. Decrease £1 by 20%.
    80 p
15. Two of the angles in a triangle are 83° and 45°.
    What is the third angle? 52°

C

1. $3 \times \boxed{8} = 24$
2. 534 455, 534 454, 534 453, $\boxed{534\,452}$
3. $100 \times 4{\cdot}15 =$ 415
4. $842 - 574 =$ 268
5. $1000 \times 14 =$ 14 000
6. $93 \div 6 = \boxed{15}$ r $\boxed{3}$
7. $37 + \boxed{23} = 60$
8. $6\frac{4}{5} - 3\frac{1}{3} =$ $3\frac{7}{15}$
9. $3^3 + 9 =$ 36
10. 192 578, 191 578, 190 578, $\boxed{189\,578}$
11. $19 - 37 =$ −18
12. $\frac{18}{6} =$ 3
13. $35 + (12 \times 4) =$ 83
14. $73 \div 4 =$ 18 r 1
15. $3{\cdot}29 + 4{\cdot}87 =$ 8·16

Can you make 573 using +, − and × and all five numbers only once

4	5
42	35
	29

$(4 \times 5) \times 29 + 35 - 42 = 573$

D

1. Write two hundred thousand point eight five in numerals. 200 000·85
2. $24 \times 8 < 28 \times 4$. True or false? false
3. Round 78·962791 to two decimal places. 78·96
4. $235{\cdot}78 \times 10 =$ 2357·8
5. Which is larger, 10^3 or 8^4? 8^4
6. Write 1250 in roman numerals. MCCL
7. Put these numbers in order, smallest first: 112·63, 121·36, 113·26 112·63, 113·26, 121·36
8. What is the square root of 144? 12
9. 2798 paintings are hanging in a gallery. 1979 of these have got flowers in them. How many paintings have no flowers on them at all? 819
10. How many cans of lemonade containing 330 ml can be filled from 2000 ml of lemonade? 6
11. What is 40% expressed as a ratio? 4:10
12. How much change from £20 do I get if I buy a video at £12·49 and 2 blank videos at £1·75 each? £4·01
13. What is the area of this shape? 76cm^2

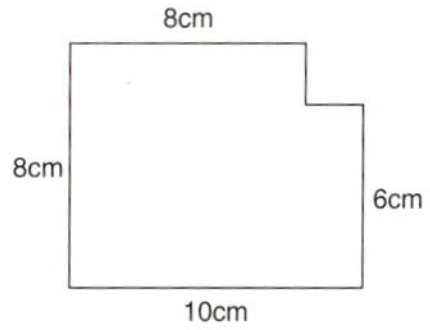

14. What is the mean average of these numbers: 5, 31, 20, 16? 18
15. There are 24 flowers in a vase. 12 are white, 8 are pink and the rest are yellow. What is the probability of a flower being yellow? 4 in 24 or $\frac{1}{6}$

Exercise 30

A

1. [7] $\times$ 7 = 49
2. 973 208, 973 209, [973 210], 973 211
3. 97 + 34 + 16 = 147
4. 467 + 554 = 1021
5. 73 $\times$ 6 = 438
6. 692 – [119] = 573
7. 73 ÷ 7 = [10] r [3]
8. $4\frac{1}{4} + 2\frac{1}{4} = 6\frac{1}{2}$
9. $\sqrt{1}$ = 1
10. [639 563], 639 547, 639 531, 639 515
11. 12 – 19 = –7
12. 12·5% = $\frac{[1]}{[8]}$ = 0·[125]
13. 140 – (9 $\times$ 5) = 95
14. 146 ÷ [24] = 6 r 2
15. $\frac{4}{9}$ of 54 = 24

Draw 3 different shapes with a perimeter of 32 cm.

B

1. Write 10 823·82 in words.
   ten thousand eight hundred and twenty-three point eight two
2. 161·16 < 116·16. True or false? false
3. I throw 3 dice. The dice show 6, 4 and 1. What is my total score for the opposite faces?
   10
4. Treble 13 plus 1, then find $\frac{1}{4}$? 10
5. 283 ÷ 100 = 2·83
6. If a compass needle moves clockwise from South-West to East, how many degrees does it move through? 225°
7. MXM in roman numerals = 1990
8. Approximately how many cm are there in a foot? 30
9. Over three weeks Bernadette saves her pocket money.
   She saves £4·97, £8·72 and £10·92.
   How much has she managed to save altogether? £24·61
10. There are 15 steps in each flight of stairs.
    Jamie climbs 7 flights.
    How many stairs has he climbed? 105
11. Four fifths of 45? 36
12. Here is a part of a timetable.

	Depart	Arrive
train A	13·59	15·08
train B	15·28	16·37

If both journeys take the same time, when did train B leave?

13. What is the perimeter of this shape? 64 cm

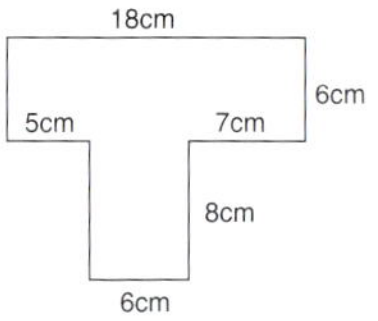

14. Decrease £19 by 10%. £17·10
15. Two of the angles in a triangle are 69° and 38°. What is the third angle? 73°

C

1 $7 \times$ 7 $= 49$

2 399 999, 400 000, 400 001, 400 002

3 $6{\cdot}01 \times 100 =$ 601

4 $731 - 642 =$ 89

5 $51 \times 10\,000 =$ 510 000

6 $175 \div 9 =$ 19 r 4

7 $59 +$ 36 $= 95$

8 $6\frac{1}{4} - 2\frac{1}{5} = 4\frac{1}{20}$

9 $3^3 - 6 =$ 21

10 379 024, 378 924, 378 824, 378 724

11 $11 - 29 =$ −18

12 $\frac{12}{9} = 1\frac{3}{9}$ or $1\frac{1}{3}$

13 $44 + (16 \times 2) =$ 76

14 $152 \div 9 =$ 16 r 8

15 $6{\cdot}58 + 5{\cdot}93 =$ 12·51

Copy and complete the Function Machine

$\div 3 - 2$

in	out
33	9
75	23
51	15
90	28
39	11
69	21
102	32
63	19
87	27

D

1 Write seven hundred and nine thousand and nine point one seven in numerals. 709 009·17

2 $369 \div 123 < 492 \div 246$. True or false? false

3 Round 107·9696962 to two decimal places. 107·97

4 $623471 \times 100 =$ 62347100

5 Which is smaller, 10^3 or 5^3? 5^3

6 Write 1997 in roman numerals. MIIIM

7 Put these numbers in order, largest first: 4·723, 6·948, 4·8, 6·8 6·948, 6·8, 4·8, 4·723

8 What is the cube root of 125? 5

9 At a soccer match there are 9752 spectators. 5685 are adults. How many are children? 4067

10 How many bunches of 11 flowers can Carole make from 190 flowers? 17

11 What is 66% expressed as a ratio? 2:3

12 How much change do I get from £20 if I buy 2 cinema tickets at £3·50 each and 2 tubs of popcorn at £1·85 each? £9·30

13 What is the area of this shape? 288 m^2

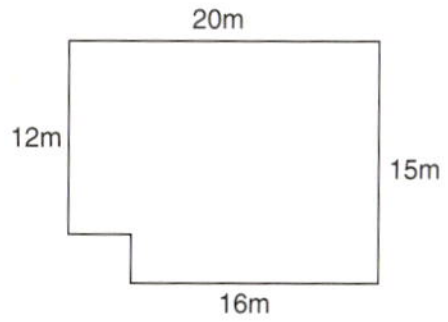

14 What is the mean average of these numbers: 11, 33, 29, 27? 25

15 There are 30 sweets in a jar. 15 are lemon, 6 are blackcurrant and the rest are lime. What is the probability of picking either a lemon or a lime sweet? 24 in 30 or $\frac{4}{5}$

Heinemann Educational Publishers
Halley Court, Jordan Hill, Oxford OX2 8EJ
a division of Reed Educational & Professional Publishing Ltd

Oxford Melbourne Auckland
Florence Prague Madrid Athens
Singapore Tokyo Sao Paulo
Chicago Portsmouth NH (USA) Mexico City
Ibadan Gaborone Johannesburg
Kampala Nairobi Kuala Lumpur

First published 1997

00 99 98 97
10 9 8 7 6 5 4 3 2

ISBN 0435 02432 9
pack of 8 pupils books: 0435 02420 5

Designed by Artistix
Typeset and illustrated by TechType, Abingdon, Oxon.
Cover design by Peter Campbell
Printed and bound by Scotprint